GRISELDA BLANCO

Cocaine Godmother

True Story of Queen of The Cartel

MAFIA LIBRARY

© **Copyright 2025 - All rights reserved.**

The content contained within this book may not be reproduced, duplicated or transmitted without direct written permission from the author or the publisher.

Under no circumstances will any blame or legal responsibility be held against the publisher, or author, for any damages, reparation, or monetary loss due to the information contained within this book, either directly or indirectly.

Legal Notice:

This book is copyright protected. It is only for personal use. You cannot amend, distribute, sell, use, quote or paraphrase any part, or the content within this book, without the consent of the author or publisher.

Disclaimer Notice:

Please note the information contained within this document is for educational and entertainment purposes only. All effort has been executed to present accurate, up to date, reliable, complete information. No warranties of any kind are declared or implied. Readers acknowledge that the author is not engaged in the rendering of legal, financial, medical or professional advice. The content within this book has been derived from various sources. Please consult a licensed professional before attempting any techniques outlined in this book.

By reading this document, the reader agrees that under no circumstances is the author responsible for any losses, direct or indirect, that are incurred as a result of the use of the information contained within this document, including, but not limited to, errors, omissions, or inaccuracies.

TABLE OF CONTENTS

Introduction 1

Chapter 1 : Early Life In Colombia 7

    Early Childhood 8

    Life In Medellin 11

    The First Crime 13

    Griselda's Attempt To Escape 15

Chapter 2 : The Path Into The Drugs World 17

    Her First Husband And Partner In Crime 18

        The Early Stage Of The Drug Empire 19

    A New Life In New York 21

    The Black Widow's First Victim 24

    A New Beginning 25

Chapter 3 : The Rise Of The Empire 27

    The Second Husband 28

    The Colombian Connection 31

    The Innovative Plan 35

    The Route Of Colombian Cocaine 39

    The Black Widow 42

    All The Power To Griselda 44

Chapter 4 : The Miami Cartel 47
The Empire Era 48
- Old Competitors, New Rivals 49
- Dea's Indirect Help 52
- The Shift In The Market 53
- Cocaine, The "Benign" Drug 55
- Miami, Griselda's Kingdom 57

The Drug Wars 58
- New Allies And Subjects 60

Plata O Plomo 63
- Hitmen And Motorcycles 64
- The Notorious Right-Hand Hitman 65

Make Way For The Queen 66

Chapter 5 : The "Cocaine Cowboys" 69
The Shootout At The Local Mall 70
The Cocaine Cowboys Reach The Headlines 75
- The Impact On Society 77

The Third Husband 80
- The Name Of The Mafia 82

New Name For The Queen—The Cocaine Godmother 83
The Higher The Climb, The Harder The Fall 88

Chapter 6 : The Downfall Of The Cocaine Queen 91
The Persecution 92
- The Obstacles To The Investigation 95

  Dea's Strategies 96
  The Arrest 98
 The Trial 99
  The Prosecution's Strategy And Griselda's Effective Defense 99
  Other Witnesses And Further Evidence 101
  The Sentence 105
 Life In Prison 106
  A Key Betrayal 106
  Griselda's Fourth Partner 109
  Griselda's Sons' Fate 111
 Back To The Starting Line 112

Chapter 7 : The End 115
 The Release 116
 Back In Medellin 118
 The Last Day 120
 Who Killed Griselda? 121
 The End 122

Conclusion 123
References 127

INTRODUCTION

Whenever you think about organized crime and cold-blooded criminals, your mind probably shows you a male figure. Films, books, series, and even the news focus on men as the main leaders of the mafia. The most renowned capo mafia are men. However, one of the bloodiest leaders of organized crime in the world, alleged to have killed over 200 people, and the mastermind of a business that made over 80 million dollars a month was a woman. In a male-dominated landscape, a ruthless, intelligent, and reckless Colombian woman built an empire that kept the most daring drug dealers on their knees. Her name was Griselda Blanco (Turner, 2024).

Also known as the Black Widow and the Cocaine Godmother, Blanco did much more than become the boss of her criminal organization. It was a male-dominated environment, and she still managed to establish a broad trading net of drugs between Latin America and the United States. Moreover, she gained so much power that she put the drug barons on their knees and forced them to follow her rules. She made them fear her more than anything else. How did a young, poor girl from Colombia become a wealthy, cruel, and manipulative criminal leader?

This journey starts in the poor barrio of Cartagena, Colombia, where Griselda had her first encounter with marginality and violence. The country, the city, and her own home were the scenarios for blood, assaults, and lives on the other side of the law. However, this book doesn't aim to redeem a life devoted to crime. Blanco was who she was. While the social context indeed shapes people's mindsets and behaviors, unlike other versions of these characters' biographies, the purpose of this story isn't either to justify their actions or even to attempt to understand them. The social background serves as the scenario where the actors play their roles.

The main purpose is to explore Griselda Blanco's story from beginning to end, highlighting the complex intertwining of ruthlessness, violence, tragedy, and a millionaire business that took her to the peak of power. We shall delve into the dark suburbs of New York and Medellin and, then, the most glamorous beaches of Miami. From a very young eye, the environment and the living conditions put her in direct contact with extreme violence. Even though we don't aim either to judge or redeem her, this context will allow us to understand not only why she came to be what she was but also how she managed to find the resources she needed to build her criminal network.

Blanco wasn't only the chief of a drug empire, the owner of a substantial fortune. She was also a mother of three children who were raised as illegal immigrants and became a byproduct of their mother's story. She was a wife, a dangerous wife who treated her couples almost as her allies or her enemies. Lastly, she was a businesswoman who found a niche—an illegal yet real niche—in the market and was skillful enough to understand the dynamics of offer and demand, trading routes, and gaps to evade the law.

Griselda Blanco has an intriguing life, from beginning to end, but also is a depiction of an era where drugs and death on the streets driven by organized crime became the preferred headlines on the news. The peak of her criminal career coincides with the progress of the drug trade in the United States and the criminal routes set by South American drug cartels via the Caribbean and Central America. As the drug traders developed their market and figured out new ways to introduce drugs into the United States, the North American country deployed strategies to block their frontiers, halt the drug market, and capture the bosses. Griselda managed to prevail over both.

While the cartels evolved, Blanco developed unique strategies that allowed her to negotiate with the other cartel bosses under her conditions. The law, meanwhile, didn't look for her as they didn't look for a woman. Eventually, her figure emerged as one of the most dangerous and wanted criminals in the world. Still, either the law or the other cartels were strong enough to dismantle her phenomenal business.

The drug trade was built in the image and likeness of Griselda Blanco. In her rise to power, she found allies and gained enemies in her homeland and in the United States. Nonetheless, she also managed to form a personal army that protected her, at least for a while. Blanco's story is full of blood, cruelty, deception, crime, and betrayal. Eventually, her empire turned from solid rocks to fading sand. Her end isn't too different from many other outlaws and criminals. She escaped the law for a long time and later paid in jail, but in the end, she met the fate she had built for herself. From the bottom to the peak, round trip, to end their days, as she probably wished the least.

Popular characters like Griselda Blanco tend to divide opinions. While for some is nothing but a cold-blooded killer, for others, she is a victim of a macabre system that pushes large sectors of society beyond the limits of law. It is the context and injustice that turn people into criminals. It is almost impossible to read about these controversial characters without being tempted to take sides. However, this book aims to provide a stark narrative of Griselda Blanco's life with no omissions or exaggerations. This is just a recount of all the details of a troubled life with many terrible consequences for individuals and countries.

As stories like Griselda's are told, myths are likely to emerge. Ideas are instilled in the audience by the media and literature. Insights shared by researchers or interviews sometimes contribute to the dissemination of fragments of stories that are half-truths or even mistaken appreciations of what happened. This on in-depth research in an attempt to debunk some myths and provide a full description of the person behind the character. Griselda Blanco doesn't need an attorney or a prosecutor. Our role here is to tell a story as it was, with as many details as possible, to inform you about this woman's life. You will feel appealed to take a side and judge by yourself, or simply read a history book that aims to shed light on a character whose name will remain in the collective memory. This book aims to provide answers to many questions that emerge when we wonder who Griselda Blanco was and why she was so feared. However, it also aims to raise new questions about the darker side of human nature and those who crossed the line to never come back.

Blanco's life was surrounded by big infamous names, men, all of them. However, Griselda was among the wealthiest and the cruelest, many times making them feel her power. How could a poor woman raised in the streets of Colombian suburbs become the most powerful drug dealer? How could such an empire crumble and let her fall victim to her own trap?

CHAPTER 1
EARLY LIFE IN COLOMBIA

Located in the North extreme of South America, Colombia is a piece of paradise on Earth. Colombia is a melting pot of different ethnic backgrounds, and also a land of deep contrasts. Its landscapes range from the impressive Andes Mountains to the warm beaches bathed by the transparent waters of the Caribbean. The air is a mixture of smells and sounds that combine the mysteries of the rainforest and the bustling cities.

During the 1940s and 1950s, massive migration waves from the rural areas to the cities deepened the issues in the urban centers. Poverty ratios increased, and that led to the escalation of violence. The unattended needs led people to feel under-represented by the traditional political parties, and the whole socio-economic system staggered.

Colombia, like many Latin American countries, passed through a period of increasing political violence. In part fueled by the emergence of the guerrilla, framed by the Cold War and the Cuban Revolution, and also by the high levels of poverty and marginality. Large sectors of the population, particularly in the most populated cities, were driven to the limits of the system. While many joined the guerrilla and engaged in rebel and terrorist activism, others became easy prey to enter criminal networks that developed in the underserved neighborhoods of the cities.

In this context, boys and girls born and raised in the suburbs of the cities were confronted with violence and exclusion at an early age. Since they had memory, they struggled to survive. They were hunted by fear, hunger, the law, and criminals. In such a context, in a poor neighborhood of Santa Marta—or Cartagena—Griselda Blanco was born.

Before exploring how she was dragged into criminal activities, we shall explore the context: the country, the city, the neighborhood, and her own family. While this overview will shed light on the main reasons why her life took that fatal course, it is not our aim to engage in a deep sociological analysis of the roots of crime. Griselda Blanco was what she was, but not paying close attention to her context would imply ignoring the set in which she played her role.

Early Childhood

The facts about Griselda Blanco's birth and early years are confusing and not well documented. It is known that she was born on February 15, 1943. By then, her country was dragged into a bloodbath, perhaps as a fateful omen of what her life would be.

By the time children start learning about the world around them, Colombia entered one of the darkest periods in its history. When Griselda Blanco was five years old, the period known as La Violencia (The Violence) was unleashed in the Colombian streets. The violence that would eventually draw her path.

La Violencia began in the 1930s with open confrontations between the political parties, but it reached its peak when the leader of the left-wing party was executed in broad daylight in the capital, Bogotá. Riots and violent attacks crowded the main cities, while the local press talked about deaths and casualties on the radio and the headlines in newspapers. The Colombian society adopted this violence as part of their social dynamics, and while they struggled to build a democratic basis, people saw death and struggle as part of the ways to seek solutions to conflicts.

During The Violence, about 190,000 people died in Colombia, making intimidation and killing just typical elements of social interaction. The logic of violence was instilled among the population, and for those with little economic resources struggling to cover the most elementary needs, it became part of daily life. Historian Elaine Carey said in her book Women Drug Traffickers that Griselda and the contemporary people grew up believing that power came from the violent (Djangi, 2024).

Colombia was one of the world's most important coffee producers and had a commodity economy based on the production and exportation of primary goods. The rise of political violence coincided with a fall in the global prices of these products, which led to the deepening of the gap between rich and poor in the country. People moved from the rural areas where making a living was getting harder and reallocated to the cities, cities that were unprepared to host thousands of new inhabitants with few resources. The newcomers settled in the suburbs of the cities and crowded into precarious neighborhoods of makeshift shelters, mainly in the suburbs.

Griselda Blanco Restrepo was born and raised in a family that moved along with the political and economic changes. There is no recorded evidence of Griselda's birthplace. However, biographers and historians have suggested that, in fact, Griselda was born in Cartagena, a city located on the northern coast around the Caribbean Sea (Biography.com Editors & Kettler, 2024). However, other sources, including one of her sons, claim that Griselda was born in Santa Marta. It is documented that she was baptized in a church in Santa Marta, and this is the only piece of evidence to trace back to the place where she was born (Tikkanen, n.d.).

Santa Marta was a beautiful, medium-sized city on the Caribbean shore of Colombia. The city was known for its important production of bananas and went through a process of expansion. However, it is possible that the Blancos didn't benefit from the business and, instead, were forced to move out. Griselda's family was very poor, and either from Santa Marta or from Cartagena, they would eventually leave. It is possible that Griselda was born in Cartagena and the family that early moved to Santa Marta. In the early 1940s, Santa Marta was a flourishing economic center, and perhaps the Blanco went there searching for better opportunities.

Little is known about Griselda's family. Her father was Fernando Blanco, but there was no reliable information about his background. Some sources suggest that Fernando wasn't Griselda's real father. This version of the story claims that Griselda's mother got pregnant by her boss, a rich man who didn't want to recognize the child and denied her his surname. This would be a reason why Griselda's mother eventually took her away from the Blanco home.

However, it is clear that the Blanco family lived in poverty. Griselda never spoke about her siblings or extended family. All that is known about her close family is her mother, Ana Lucía Restrepo, who was her only tight close during Griselda's early childhood and played a significant role in shaping her life (queerstorian, 2019).

Life in Medellin

The first years of childhood are key to any child's development. It is the period of life with a greater impact on the individual's psychological and cognitive development. During the first years of life until eight years old, children learn the first concepts to understand the world and build life skills, such as self-confidence and socialization. Positive experiences and a nurturing environment will create a path of healthy development, while a negative environment will possibly have a detrimental impact on physical, social, and emotional development (Why Early Childhood Matters, n.d.).

The time between birth and three years old is critical. During this period, the child's brain establishes billions of neuron connections and creates the first images of reality. Parents or other caregivers became the main source of safety and support that will promote positive input for this process (Why Early Childhood Matters, n.d.). Mothers and fathers are supposed to take care of little children and ensure they feel safe.

This was not the case for Griselda. Something wasn't right within her family during this critical stage of her life. There is no official record of the family history, but it is known that Griselda's mother took her daughter and left her husband. By then, they were living in

Santa Marta. Ana Lucía and young Griselda moved from a pleasant and relatively quiet coastal city to one of the Colombian largest and most populated cities, Medellin.

Medellin is located in the southwest of the country in the Antioquia district, a name that would become popular for becoming the center of the drug cartel's activities. By the end of the 1940s, Medellin had turned from a large town into a large and noisy city, one of the epicenters of the economic and political landscapes in times when this wasn't precisely an advantage. According to Ponti (2020), Medellin was considered the most dangerous city in the world.

Griselda's new home was the second city in Colombia and became a preferred target for people from rural areas and nearby cities, probably looking for jobs or better living conditions. Instead, the Colombians that reached the big city found themselves compelled to settle as they could in the underserved neighborhoods. That was the case of Griselda and her mother.

Settled in their new home, Griselda and her mother lived in extreme poverty. Ana Lucía was a sexual worker who engaged in substance abuse and violent episodes. Some accounts state that she took her clients to the house where she lived with her daughter. Griselda grew up not only as a witness to her mother's activity but also as a frequent victim of her clients.

Griselda spent all her childhood, from when she was three until she escaped from her mother's house, being physically abused by the men who visited her mother. She was sexually abused and frequently beaten, and some sources even suggest that her mother used her as part of her activities. It is unknown if Griselda went to school or ever visited a doctor as any typical child.

To stay away from this cruel treatment, Griselda tried to spend most of her time in the streets. These streets were no man's land. The violence that dominated the country was depicted in every corner of the neighborhood. Drugs and crime were common, and the concept of law and order was nonexistent. At a very young age, Griselda joined the gangs in her neighborhood.

Forced by the circumstances, she learned to navigate and adapt to the unwritten rules of the street, different from the legal system which, by the way, was engulfed in chaos and incapable of bringing solutions either to poverty or violence. This doesn't mean Griselda didn't have the choice to become a good citizen, but it does depict the landscape where she had to figure out how to survive.

The First Crime

Ever since she was three until she became a teenager, Griselda divided her time between being her mother's clients' victims and the street gangs. She was driven to crime at a very young age, even though there are no criminal records for those years. Different accounts point out that being a child, Griselda was involved in many small crimes, such as theft, petty, and other criminal activities.

Griselda befriended local low-criminals, probably the way to survive in the streets. She resorted to these petty crimes to earn some money. One of the most typical activities was smuggling. She didn't smuggle drugs yet; instead, it was perfume from Venezuela (Ponti, 2020). While the load and amounts of money were limited, it was the first incursion of a criminal endeavor that, in the near future, would turn Griselda into a feared criminal.

Besides these relatively small crimes, Griselda would have a notorious debut in crime, setting the stage for the cold-blooded and cruel murderer she would become later. Griselda was only 11 years old and had lived nothing a girl of that age should have lived. She never had toys or enjoyed child games with friends. She didn't know what feeling safe and loved was. It isn't that weird that this young Griselda looked at the world in anger and contempt. However, it is impressive to learn that such a young girl could get involved in a major crime.

She couldn't have done it alone, though there are no accounts of who accompanied her in planning and executing the crime. She and probably a gang reached a rich neighborhood and kidnapped a 10-year-old boy. The kid was playing outside and Griselda and her companions waited for a moment when he was left alone and helpless. They took the boy to the suburbs and phoned the family to demand a reward.

Kidnapping and blackmailing are big crimes for an 11-year-old girl; nonetheless, it is believed that Griselda was the mind and the boss of the operation. The child's family refused to pay the ransom and instead went to the police to intervene. Griselda's gang was cornered. In those circumstances, Griselda showcased not only her disposition to becoming a gang leader but also her irrepressible violence and cruelty.

When they knew that there would be no money and instead they would eventually be confronted with the police, Griselda made a drastic decision. She took a gun, pointed it at the child's head, and shot him. The boy fell down dead. Griselda didn't hesitate. She didn't ask for permission or thought about the consequences. The boy was almost her age, but there was no room for pity in her mind. She was only 11, and she was already a killer.

This first crime was probably a point of no return for Griselda. Her early years had planted the seed of violence within her, and this terrible at such an early age only confirmed it. The situation at home didn't change, so Griselda spent more and more time on the streets. She became a prostitute seeking for means of survival and remained a smuggler and theft. She added other crimes to her record, many of them simple robberies in the street and others more elaborated as documents forgery (Djanggi, 2024). These activities led her to meet the man she would join for another chapter in her life.

Despite these minor offenses, the path for major crimes was set. After the kidnapping and execution of the boy, Griselda became a popular name among the local criminals. They started calling her "*la patrona*" (the boss). This first murder was a sort of baptism of fire that proved Griselda her tempering to take others' lives and show herself she definitely had no limits. It was her time to be violent then.

Griselda's Attempt to Escape

When Griselda was 14 years old, she decided that she had had enough of the violence experienced by her mother's side. Being a teenager, Griselda wasn't an innocent girl. Her innocence had long been stolen by her rough living conditions. A family that couldn't protect her, a system that neglected her and pushed her to live on its margins, and the streets that welcomed her just to take her to the darkest sides of society.

Griselda was perhaps trying to escape from the monsters in her house. In the streets, she met people who introduced her to crime. What did she know about good or wrong? One of those who met became her protector. We can imagine that she fell in love or thought that, for once, she would have someone to protect her. Or perhaps she just found a ticket to freedom or what she thought would be an opportunity for a better life.

His name was Carlos Trujillo, and 14-year-old Griselda ran away with the man who would be her first husband and also her first partner in crime.

CHAPTER 2
THE PATH INTO THE DRUGS WORLD

After a childhood marked by hardships and abuse, Griselda Blanco ran away from her mother's house when she was only 14. By then, she wasn't a child anymore. The circumstances put her on the streets and trained her to survive. Nonetheless, there was something in her spirit that didn't conform to survival. The traumatic events she went through since she had memory planted a seed of evil inside her. Perhaps she went out to the streets looking for revenge, to make the world pay for what she had suffered. Perhaps she wanted to eliminate anything and anyone who could threaten her. Maybe she wanted to take control of her surroundings before it turned against her. Or maybe it was just the only way she knew about good or wrong: "Wrong: I die; good: anything that serves to keep me alive."

When she ran away from home, Griselda already had a criminal record and a name of her own as a renowned criminal in her neighborhood. She had escalated from minor theft to smuggling and forging documents and had even killed a person—a child. Roaming Medellin's suburban streets as a sexual worker, she teamed up with a man who was engaged in the same criminal activities. He became her partner and husband.

Her First Husband And Partner In Crime

Griselda met Carlos Trujillo when she was 13. He was probably one of her clients. Carlos had quite a reputation as a forger and might have introduced Griselda to the business. This activity would become a gateway from Colombia to new horizons. The critical economic situation in Colombia led many Colombians to migrate, and the preferred destination was the United States. The North American country had many requirements for outsiders, and migrants relied on illegal documentation. That was the starting point for Trujillo's business.

The papers he could provide and his knowledge of the routes and processes to make it successfully into the U.S. borders gave Trujillo a share of powers. People in the marginalized areas reached out to him to help them leave the country, and Trujillo facilitated the means to migrate. That was also a good source of income for him.

Within a short time, Trujillo became a mentor to Griselda. He initiated her not only in this crime, but also opened a new gate into smuggling. Until then, Griselda had smuggled perfumes and other minor things. After getting married to him, Griselda entered Trujillo's other criminal network. He had started smuggling drugs to later distribute them in the streets. Despite being a newcomer and just a teenager, Griselda quickly learned the dynamics of the market. Soon, she would bring in some terrible innovative ideas.

Amidst a life devoted to crime, Griselda Blanco and Carlos Trujillo got married. It is impossible to know if they were moved by love, need, or desperation. Griselda was much younger than him, yet it doesn't necessarily mean that he exerted much power over her.

Griselda wasn't an ordinary teenager. By the time she got married, she had lived a thousand lives in Medellin streets.

Trujillo became an important person in Griselda's life, not only because he was her mentor for more complex criminal activities. He was her first husband and father of her three children: Dixon, Uber, and Osvaldo Trujillo Blanco. When she gave birth to her third son, Griselda was only 21 years old. Her children would be raised surrounded by the agitated life outside the law of their parents. Eventually, this would mark their future as it once happened to their mother. All of them turned into criminals and had violent deaths. But let's not bring it forward.

The Early Stage of the Drug Empire

Mother of three, Griselda didn't relegate her endeavors to the street. Trujillo and Griselda had established a smuggling network of a drug that was becoming increasingly popular among the poor sectors of the Medellin population and was taken on the streets: marijuana. Griselda and Carlos didn't introduce marihuana in the city, nor did they invent the business. They just had the time to realize where the underground market was going and had the resources to take advantage of a network that was built almost two decades ago.

In the late 1950s and the early 1960s, drug traffic wasn't a highly organized activity. The most popular drug by then was marihuana, and its consumption was progressively increasing in the United States as part of a counter-culture practice. The burst of the Cuban Revolution in 1959 had raised the alarm of a rebel movement of Latin immigrants in the United States, and smoking marijuana spread among the potential rebels in special social groups such as university students, rock 'n' roll enthusiasts, and the emerging hippie movement.

In the next years, the peace movement against the Vietnam War expanded this social movement and spread a prospective market for drugs. Some scholars allege that access to drugs was somehow facilitated by authorities as it contributed to appeasing the spirits of the rebels. The act of rebellion was to enter a distorted reality by the use of hallucinogenics rather than by taking up arms against the system (Sáenz Rovner, 2007). Colombia became the main producer and provider of marijuana.

The connection between Colombian marihuana producers and the United States was actually driven by a trading channel built during World War II to avoid the Nazi restrictions on coffee cargo. By the 1960s, marijuana was camouflaged within the coffee cargo and entered the country as any other commodity. This intensified marihuana production in Colombia to supply an expanding demand in the United States (*Marijuana Boom*, 2020). However, not all the marijuana production was for exportation; part of it was allocated to the local market.

In the 1960s and 1970s, Colombian main urban centers became important markets for marihuana domestic consumption. Some scholars highlight to debunk the hypothesis of Colombia being a victim of an externally induced phenomenon (Sáenz Rovner, 2007). Nonetheless, it must be pointed out that while coffee, cotton, and bananas—legal commodities—were produced by the traditional wealthy landlords, the production of marihuana became an opportunity for marginalized groups, mainly concentrated in the Magdalena region (*Marijuana Boom*, 2020).

Medellin is located in the Antioquia province within the Magdalena region. This means Griselda and Trujillo were placed at one of the epicenters of the marihuana production with access to one of the largest markets considering it was the second most populated city of Colombia. Trujillo already managed some threads of the underworld market and had connections in the United States. So, the evident next step in their criminal raid was engaging in marihuana smuggling.

A New Life in New York

In 1964, the Blanco-Trujillo duo moved to the United States. Some sources suggest that they were looking for new horizons where to expand their business. Other researchers took from diverse testimonials that they had to leave Medellin because they had gotten into trouble. In other words, they didn't move, but fled from Colombia.

To leave the country, Griselda and her husband had to take fake names and use their own services. Trujillo provided forged documentation to his wife and children. It is relevant to note that by this time, Griselda and Trujillo weren't public figures, and the law wasn't actually looking for them. If they were running away, it was probably from a gang feud with other criminals like them. Moreover, identification processes weren't still so sophisticated, and there wasn't an institution aimed at organized crime persecution. This illustrates that the drug market was still at its emerging stage, which will allow us to consider Griselda Blanco one of the pioneers.

With no recorded inconveniences, Griselda and her family settled in New York City. As it had been in other historical periods for European migrants, New York was the preferred destination for those trying to escape from poverty in Latin American countries. Large communities from Puerto Rico, Dominican Republic, Ecuador, and Colombia, among others, crowded in the marginalized areas of the metropolitan region. According to records, 86% of the Latinos settled in New York in the 1960s. Over time, they moved to nearby cities, but 50% remained (Bergad, 2020).

The situation of the newly arrived was critical. They lived in terrible conditions, with little access to essential services and almost no resources to cover their basic needs. This environment created conducive circumstances for the development of crime and substance abuse. Where the state doesn't reach, and people struggle to survive, the limits between good and wrong are blurred, and the sense of order loses sense.

Over 800,000 foreign people settled in New York in the 1960s, most of them without legal documentation (McMahon, 2011). During President Kennedy's tenure, a migration policy reformation opened more opportunities for Latino migrants. This led to a dramatic rise of immigrants coming from Latin American countries, raising concern and xenophobia among the U.S. citizens (*The History of Immigration Policies in the U.S.*, n.d.). Despite the new legal frame, many immigrants couldn't prove any affiliation with resident citizens who waited for them. Thus, they remained undocumented and thus, unable to seek stable jobs. In this context, there were large sectors of the population not only living in critical conditions but also building their lives on the margins of the law.

Trujillo and Griselda, both illegal immigrants, used this as an opportunity to start a business in their new hometown. They used their skills to forge IDs and sell them to the desperate Latino undocumented immigrants. Nonetheless, they soon realized that the context in the poor neighborhoods of New York resembled those in Medellin. The streets were full of young people with little hope for their futures, raised amidst violence, as Griselda did. They were an easy target for substances, and marihuana had already reached the stage.

Thus, Trujillo and Griselda took another step into the criminal landscape in the new city. They had already experienced smuggling marihuana in Medellin, and they replicated the system in New York. They were aware of some trafficking routes, and it didn't take long for them to build their own network. There were already other drug dealers in New York City, and all of them were men. Nonetheless, Griselda didn't let them intimidate her, and soon, she would find a way to keep the business for herself and reach an advantageous position ahead of her competitors.

A short time after they settled in New York, Griselda and Trujillo got divorced. The motivations aren't clear. However, it is known that they remained partners in the marihuana business. Griselda was an undocumented Latino woman raising three children in the dark side of the capital of the world. She had little resources and were all linked to crime. She had few options ahead.

The Black Widow's First Victim

Not long after the divorce, Trujillo died. There are several versions surrounding his death. Some sources highlight that he had many complex health issues. He indeed had cirrhosis, and it was argued that he eventually died of his disease. Nonetheless, other strong versions suggest that Trujillo was, in fact, Griselda's first victim as the Black Widow, as she would be called later: All of her husbands had a violent death (Shilliday, 2024).

It is believed that Trujillo and Griselda had a disagreement over the outcome of a business. Something upset Griselda; perhaps Trujillo didn't follow her orders, or she didn't get all of her money. In any case, Griselda ordered one of her men to pay a visit to Trujillo and execute him.

Griselda was never charged for Trujillo's death, but it doesn't mean she was innocent of his death. It is true that Trujillo was shot by a hitman, not by his wife, but it doesn't mean she didn't give the order. Anyway, there was no proof against her. Trujillo had collected enemies on his own, so it isn't impossible that his death was mistakenly credited to her ambitious and cruel wife.

Some versions, however, account that Griselda herself once confessed to having sent her people to execute him, but it was extra-official and had no legal importance. After having Trujillo dead—by any or another means—, Griselda moved out of New York to Miami.

A New Beginning

By 1970, the landscape had changed. The drug business was on an upward curve. The social context of conflict and unrest was heating up, and the levels of drug consumption were increasing. The United States had increased the control in the borders to stop the influx of undocumented people but also of drugs, as it was getting out of their control.

Meanwhile, a new substance was infiltrating the market and becoming quickly popular. It was a white powder more powerful than marijuana. It was cocaine.

The new merchandise was an opportunity for Griselda. She had no studies and had always relied on her instincts to survive. However, she had a great sense of opportunity and demonstrated to be resourceful and highly skilled in business. She had the "nose" to find market niches and the ability to create the resources to turn them into success. She early saw cocaine's potential and envisioned innovative ways to flood the U.S. market with it.

Perhaps it was her sharp sense of business that suggested her move to Miami. The peninsula would soon become the main entrance gate of drugs to the United States. Its strategic position on the Mexican Gulf and direct connection to Latin America made it the perfect place for a drug empire headquarters. However, Griselda still had a lot to do before becoming the cocaine queen.

Shortly after relocating to Miami, Griselda met her second husband. He was a seasoned Colombian drug dealer with many relevant and also dangerous connections to the local cartels back in the Magdalena Region. Hard to say if Griselda picked her husbands for the "business" opportunities or for any romantic motivations. What is certain is that her new acquisition and her new home moved her to redesign her strategy.

However, not everything flew smoothly for her. She had to get rid of her other husband, and that became a modus operandi in her career: Anyone who hampered her interests was simply eliminated. Moreover, she wasn't only fighting against her competitors to secure the lead spot in the market; the United States engaged in a program to seek out and stop drug dealers. She would have to take care of her back from then on.

CHAPTER 3
THE RISE OF THE EMPIRE

Life for immigrants has never been easy, but Griselda didn't stay in the place of a victim. Instead, she managed to make it the base of her business. She found the weaknesses in the system and used them to her benefit. A Colombian woman in her 20s with three children to raise on her own could have collapsed. Instead, she relied on her skills and resources acquired from her first husband and early experiences to start building what would become the largest and most powerful empire in the drug market.

She transformed each disadvantage into a tool to strengthen her position. As an illegal immigrant, she had found a way to become important to this community, gaining power and influence. Besides, this gave her a thorough understanding of how this underground world worked and what people in it needed. Griselda grew up on the margins of society and was aware of how much people are willing to risk when they have nothing to lose.

Moreover, her troubled experiences with men deterred her from waiting for a Charming Prince to rescue her. Instead, somehow, she decided that men would be just something to use and discharge according to her plans. That happened to her first husband, Trujillo.

He was the gateway to leave Colombia and learn the ins and outs of forging. He was also her first partner to smuggle small amounts of marijuana and lay the grounds for a major market. When he wasn't useful anymore and turned into an obstacle, she simply got rid of him.

Her relationship with Trujillo and how it ended was just the precedent of a troubled relationship with men. Even Griselda's sons were reached by this complexity since they were soon involved in their mother's murky activities. They were dragged to tragedy either by their mother's acts or omissions. After getting divorced and having her first husband's death, Griselda was ready to move on and find a new partner.

However, not only the men in Griselda's life were part of her criminal strategy. Her second husband was one a piece of a larger gear that involved the most important and dangerous drug landlords. Each of them ruled within their own networks, but Griselda managed to put all of them under her influence. Her keen strategy included showing no mercy to display how far she would reach and a timely and innovative vision to unlock untapped resources.

The Second Husband

Griselda met her next husband, Alberto Bravo, while she still lived in New York. She had recently divorced Trujillo, though he wasn't dead yet. It isn't confirmed if Griselda had started her relationship with Bravo before the marriage with Trujillo was actually over. Griselda had made the most of Trujillo and was looking for a way to upgrade her economic potential. She was no longer interested in low profitable businesses; she had something greater in mind.

Alberto Bravo was a Colombian drug dealer who had close connections with an emerging criminal organization. Like others, Bravo started smuggling marijuana into the United States. Nonetheless, in the early 1970s, marijuana was being replaced by a new type of drug: cocaine.

Bravo's providers were Colombian drug traffickers who, in the 1970s, shifted production to this new and more profitable product. These traffickers evolved and shaped cartels, "illicit consortiums of independent organizations formed to limit competition and control the production and distribution of illegal drugs. Drug cartels are extremely well-organized, well-financed, efficient, and ruthless," according to Encyclopedia Britannica (Samuels, n.d., para. 1).

When Griselda met Bravo, he was already smuggling small quantities of cocaine provided by the Colombian cartels. It was the origin of a large, violent, and sophisticated criminal organization. The United States was already aware of the threat. During Richard Nixon's tenure, the state began the war on drugs in 1968. Nonetheless, this seemed to have created conducive conditions for drug trafficking to expand. By 1975, the Colombian traffickers introduced cocaine within suitcases. It is important to highlight that the control systems and technology in airports were still precarious, so they succeeded in going unnoticed. At that moment, "cocaine could be processed for $1500/kilo in jungle labs and could be sold on the streets of America for as much as $50,000/kilo" (The Colombian Cartels, n.d., para. 2).

Bravo was part of this trafficking net. His part of the business had two main headquarters: Medellin, where the main drug landlords were established. The other center was New York, where he received the cocaine cargo and used dealers to distribute the drug in the streets.

Even though the amounts and revenues were still modest if compared to the astronomical levels it would reach, Bravo was an international player, and that was convenient for Griselda. It is impossible to judge her feelings toward Bravo, yet it is clear that her main motivations weren't romantic or emotional, as facts would prove later.

Alberto Bravo introduced Griselda to the world of cocaine, and she quickly saw the potential. He was also her initial link to the Medellin Cartel. Without Bravo, Griselda would have needed another route to get in touch with the main cocaine providers in the North American market. Shortly after, the couple moved to Queens and continued their endeavors in their new neighborhood.

Within a short time, Griselda and Bravo set the cocaine business in motion. The initial shipments that came from Medellin were purchased to nurses who worked in a clinic in the city. Bravo had an import-export company that Bravo ran with his brother (Freixes, 2024). Among the products, they traded women's clothes. The business served both to display the initial logistics for the new business and also to act as a screen to cover the illegal activities.

At first, Griselda and Bravo followed the Colombian dealer's modus operandi and used suitcases to introduce the drugs. Then, they used the company's clothes packages. However, as drug consumption rose on the streets, the controls became more exhaustive. Griselda was the mastermind behind an ingenious initiative that established a terrible precedent that would be imitated by drug dealers all over the world.

In the early stages of Griselda and Bravos' business, they were able to sell cocaine ten times its value on the streets of New York (Freixes, 2024). Soon, the couple decided to move to Miami. Sources don't provide details about the motivations for shifting their base of operations, but it was definitely a strategic move. Miami became the core of the business for its geographical position.

The Colombian Connection

Griselda and Bravo were doing a good job, first in New York and later in Miami. They had assembled a solid distribution net and had an expanding customer base. The couple contributed to the success of the drug market and made it more attractive to Colombian stakeholders. The decade of the 1970s saw the rise of the Medellin cartel becoming the main drug producer and trafficker of the world for many years. Only over a decade later, its power would be overshadowed by the Cali cartel and the Mexican dealers late in the 1980s. Even then, the Medellin cartel remained a powerful group.

As the profits rose, more people were attracted to join the business in Colombia. The main stakeholders were Jose Gonzalo Rodriguez Gacha. Before entering cocaine trafficking, they were engaged in illegal emerald trading. Soon, the Ochoa brothers entered the game. Juan David, Jorge, and Fabio Ochoa came from a wealthy and respected family. They had raised a fortune through ranching and horsing. The business was used as a facade to hide the money coming from the drug trade and served to explain the outstanding increase in their accounts. Later, Pablo Escobar joined the group. Originally, he was a street theft, but he quickly became the mastermind of the criminal organization.

Alongside these main characters, a key player at the beginning was Carlos Lehder. He was one of the leaders and the one who designed the logistics to take larger cargoes of cocaine from the production centers in South America to the United States. Before cocaine, Lehder had already established the routes to smuggling marijuana, and later, he shifted to cocaine. He later implemented small airplanes for cocaine shipments to overcome the logistic obstacles and revolutionize the drug trade. The aircraft could fly at low altitudes and avoid being detected by the radars, which made it almost impossible to be tracked. It was also Lehder who added an island in the Bahamas to triangulate the connection between the Colombian crops and labs and the base in Miami. He bought the island to use it as the cartel's main trading point. The planes could recharge fuel on the island, and eventually, it would serve to store the drugs. It enabled the cartel to transport larger shipments and, thus, increase their profits exponentially.

As the business grew, Pablo Escobar became the leader of the cartel, known for his unlimited violence. He became a public figure and displayed different strategies to confront the local authorities, always hiding the drug trade behind the screen of licit businesses such as selling livestock. As the cartel gained power, the confrontation with the Colombian government became more violent. It is estimated that the Medellin Cartel was responsible for the death of over 110.000 people—including over 5,000 members of the police and the Colombian army—between its emergence in the middle 1970s and Escobar's death in 1993 (Cubis, 2017). The Medellin Cartel's shock force can't be separated from the economic power driven by the sophisticated and effective supply chain they developed.

The cocaine was originally produced in Bolivia and manufactured in laboratories established in the Colombian jungle. From there, cocaine was retailed to the United States, where trading leaders like Griselda Blanco and Alberto Bravo distributed it. Griselda and Bravo didn't only own the streets. They became a key element in this complex supply chain. They provided the market where to allocate the cocaine shipment and ensured safe access for the illegal cargo to the United States. In fact, while Griselda and Bravo benefited from the Medellin cartel taking them as main providers for an expanding market, Escobar and the Ochoa brothers found in Griselda the way to access a new market. Before they established such a bond, the Medellin Cartel had only traded cocaine in Colombia and smuggled modest quantities to Ecuador through the border. Griselda offered the cartel a not-inconsiderable opportunity to escalate the business.

Even though in the early 1970s, the drug trade was incipient, the United States had declared war on drugs. Nixon had announced it in 1968, but in 1970, Congress passed the Controlled Substances Act. The next year, the president declared that drugs had become "a national emergency" and appointed drugs as the "public enemy number one." Since then, the use of drugs has become a crime, and the government displayed strict measures for crimes related to drug trafficking. Two years later, the Drug Enforcement Agency (DEA) was formed, especially targeted at drug crimes, from drug possession and distribution to major crimes such as smuggling.

This framed a new scenario for drug dealers, which eventually consolidated Griselda's power in relation to the Colombian and other cartels. One of the drug dealers' greatest concerns was to be captured in their countries but extradited to the United States, where they would be judged under these strict laws enacted during Nixon's presidency. Griselda wasn't concerned about that, and she moved like a fish in the water in the United States. It was her land then.

When Griselda moved to Miami, she and her husband became the cornerstone of the business. She could control the market from the inside and facilitated the access routes to the Colombian traffickers. This gave Griselda power over them, even when they commanded their own armies in Colombia, they needed her to introduce the cocaine in the US with low costs that made the business more profitable and safer. While the Colombian traffickers found a way to press the local government to avoid extradition, they relied on Griselda to sustain the market.

Griselda and Bravo hadn't completely gone unnoticed by the authorities. In fact, in early 1975, Griselda, her husband, and the other 30 people who worked for them were indicted on federal drug conspiracy charges. The U.S. government launched what was known as Operation Banshee and was behind Griselda's trace. It was the largest case related to cocaine trafficking case in history.

To escape from going to jail, Griselda and Bravo decided to return to Colombia. In April 1975, they took a plane and landed in

Medellin, where they would continue with their business while they waited for things to calm down. During her time in Medellin, Griselda strengthened ties with the Colombian bosses. By then, they respected and feared her.

The Innovative Plan

Griselda made two consecutive moves: she shifted her husband and embarked on a new business. She had carefully studied the market and realized that the greater profits came from cocaine rather than marijuana. She also explored the alternatives to introduce the drugs into the United States. Before Lehder supplied the Medellin Cartel with private aircraft, Griselda came up with another simpler plan to smuggle in cocaine using the resources they already had.

She introduced an innovative strategy as an alternative to the suitcases. She saw the potential of the clothes import and export and thought about smuggling drugs in a way nobody would suspect. She used her husband's licit female clothes store and hired women who traveled from Colombia to the United States. Initially, she hired women who were supposed to be fashion models who would participate in advertising the company's brands of clothes and accessories.

They were all gorgeous young women who traveled all together to take part in fashion shows and photo shoots for advertising campaigns. What nobody knew was that in the seams of their lingerie, they carried the illegal substance. Griselda had invented the "mules" (Freixes, 2024).

The mules were originally women used by drug dealers to introduce drugs through the frontiers without being unnoticed. The mules became a common practice for drug smuggling all over the world and are still popular at present. The term was taken from mules used by traffickers to transport goods for trading. In fact, drug trafficking and mules were used in Asia early in the 20th century. Mules are bred from donkeys and horses that can easily move through rugged terrain and are capable of carrying heavy loads. They were typically used in Southeast Asia (Thailand, Burma, and Laos) to transport opium, a narcotic taken from poppy plants grown by local farmers (*Drug Mule Bell and Bridle*, n.d.).

Griselda might have never heard about these mules, and even though the concept was already linked to drug smuggling, she is credited to have invented the concept of drug mules in the Western world (*Drug Mule Bell and Bridle*, n.d.). Later, drug dealers around the world implemented the strategy.

In the early 1970s, when Griselda started using "mules," the control systems at airports weren't as evolved as they are in the present. Technology was just developing the first X-ray screening to control the luggage. However, it wasn't an exhaustive inspection. The passengers were checked superficially with an electronic magnetometer, which was later replaced with metal detectors (Berti, 2020). These tools mainly aimed to detect weapons or explosives but were useless to detect cocaine within the model's lingerie.

These were primitive basic systems regarding the clarity of the images and the ability to detect drugs. Jeffrey Hamel, CEO of IDSS, the company that provides high-tech screen scanners at present, explained (*Technological Advances Take Airport X-Ray*, 2022) that these scanners failed because they each used a single stationary X-ray detector, providing the inspector with just one view of the baggage's interior. They just took a single shot through the piece of luggage, with objects inside the bag obscuring the X-ray's path and creating shadows, and that's how airport security had to judge what was inside your bag (para. 4).

Almost 20 years later, a new scanner device was invented. At present, airports have integrated scanning systems with highly skilled professionals who have the devices that take high-quality 3D images, and the set of skills to make accurate interpretations (Technological Advances Take Airport X-Ray, 2022).

Griselda had a vision for the business and realized how to take advantage of the weaknesses of the system. When the first mules passed through the airport scanners without revealing the cocaine in the clothes, Griselda decided to risk even more. She didn't only pack the cocaine in the seams of the women's underwear. She started adding secret compartments, like inside pockets, to the lingerie to increase the amount of drugs carried by each mule.

The women were never discovered. According to the Miami New Times, Griselda and the mules system revolutionized smuggling. Back in Medellin, Griselda opened a factory where she could control the production of custom-made bras and girdles, which she later used with her mules to transport cocaine into the United States. Griselda's chain supply enabled her to produce and import 3,400 lb (1,450 kilograms) of cocaine a month (Merryweather, 2018).

By the middle 1970s, Griselda and Bravo had expanded their dealer network and hired 1,500 people to use as mules and in their manufacturing facilities. According to records, the couple earned millions of dollars a month. Soon, the connection with the Medellin cartel, mainly led by Pablo Escobar, paid off. Griselda and Bravo hired their own pilots to use aircraft to smuggle cocaine into the US (LeGardye, 2024).

As the business progressed and the revenues multiplied, Griselda and Bravo continued to expand their mules network. In the following years, they didn't only use beautiful young women to transport the drug. After the first cargoes passed through the scanners in the airports, Griselda became more confident and increased the load of each mule's secret package. Later, she didn't need the screen of models and fashion shows, and besides them, she and her husband hired anyone who would be ready to risk their life in exchange for some money.

Men, women, and children, anyone would be a good prospect to serve Griselda's interests. All of them were in extremely vulnerable conditions and needed money to survive. Many others were in trouble or already owed favors to Griselda or Bravo. In those cases, mules weren't "hired" but compelled to work for them. Even though Griselda gave these people money—a good amount of money—they weren't completely free to choose.

This way, Griselda started developing a modus operandi that would be the basis of her empire and later imitated by other criminal organizations. Griselda used money and violence as the main means to subjugate people, buying their loyalty and taking their lives in her hands.

The Route of Colombian Cocaine

Cocaine derives from the coca plant, an indigenous species of the Andean region in South America, particularly in Bolivia and Peru. Originally, Native people grew coca to mitigate the effects of high altitudes, for social and religious rituals, and also as a hallucinogen. Thus, the beginning of the coca harvest didn't begin with the attempt to produce and export drugs. Also, for these contextual reasons, the early crops of coca didn't ring the alarms of the local governments.

The Colombian drug dealers saw a new niche in the U.S. drug market in the 1970s when cocaine was becoming popular as a symbol of the glamorous life of musicians and celebrities. While marijuana was a cheap drug associated with the lower segments of society, cocaine was perceived as a symbol of status. It was more expensive due to a more complex process of manufacturing and because it was still difficult to get. The Colombian traffickers of the Medellin cartel saw this as an opportunity to develop a massive wealthy business.

The Medellin cartel benefited from its proximity to the coca plant harvesting locations. The first step was to increase the growth of this crop. The local farmers were forced to multiply coca plant crops either under coercion or economic necessity.

However, cultivating coca plants was just the first step. It had to undergo a chemical manufacturing process that turned the coca leaves into coca paste, and for that, dealers required laboratories. The Medellin cartel established their laboratories in the heart of the Amazon jungle in the Colombian territory. The leafy vegetation allowed them to keep the laboratories hidden and were undetected by the authorities for years.

The Medellin cartel established the main laboratory in the jungle area of the Caquetá and Meta departments in Colombia, near the border with Ecuador. It was an easy and safe access to receive the raw material from Bolivia and Peru. Also, this proximity made Ecuador the first target for the Colombian traffickers. However, when the Medellin cartel approached Griselda and Bravo, they saw an easy entrance gate to the United States.

Then, they developed a new system to transport the cocaine already processed into the United States. Griselda was already using the mules system to transport minor loads within the women's clothes. When Griselda and the Medellin cartel engaged in a somewhat collaborative business, they combined different methods. Nonetheless, the new system didn't fully replace Griselda's method.

The Medellin cartel started using aircraft and boats to take the drugs from the Colombian northern shore to the United States. The closest accessible point was the Florida peninsula, where Griselda had her headquarters in Miami.

As the business grew, the cartel needed more means of transportation and more sophisticated logistics. Lehder bought an island in the Bahamas and the Medellin cartel used Norman's Cay as a base where the planes could recharge fuel. Due to its proximity, Norman's Cay and Miami became the epicenter of the drug market in the late 1970s until 1983. Later, Lehder had to give up Norman's Cay, and the Medellin cartel had to shift its route. Then, they made a new connection through Panama (Catiang, 2018).

In the late 1970s, Colombian-processed cocaine was distributed in the most important cities of the United States: Los Angeles, New York, and Miami, which became the hubs for further dissemination of the drug across the country. However, Miami became the capital of the drug empire, and there, the Blanco-Bravo couple were the emperors.

As the master of the drug business in Miami, Griselda had a close and complex relationship with the Medellin cartel boss, Pablo Escobar. They needed each other: Griselda had her own facilities in Medellin, but the amounts she produced were much lower than Escobar's production in La Tranquilina. Meanwhile, Escobar needed Griselda to allocate all that production to a profitable market. The connection between the two of them swung from partnership to rivalry. Neither of them wanted to resign power or wealth.

There are many versions of the type of relationship Griselda had with Escobar, though neither of them is solidly backed up with evidence. What is certain is that they indeed met. He had traveled to Miami in the late 1970s (there is no precise data of the year) especially to meet Griselda. By then, he was just starting with the drug business, and Griselda was already the master. Escobar wanted to enter the game in the United States, and Griselda saw the potential of what he could bring to her endeavors. It is worth noticing that Escobar was still a teenager, and Griselda was in her early 20s (Presnell, 2024).

Even though they needed each other, their interests usually overlapped, and the relationship wasn't free of violence and tension. Escobar was a dreadful drug dealer who would mercilessly execute rival dealers, allies who deviated from his orders, policemen, and innocent people. However, he respected and feared Griselda (Córdoba, 2024).

The Black Widow

Griselda and Alberto Bravo had fled from the United States in 1975 because the DEA was behind them. This means that by that time, when the Medellin cartel was still emerging, Griselda had increased her operations enough to call the authorities' attention (Biography.com Editors & Kettler, S., 2024). Once in Colombia, the couple used Bravo's connection with the Medellin Cartel. However, the criminal duo wouldn't last long.

After their arrival in Colombia, Griselda and Bravo settled in Medellin but occasionally traveled to other cities. They were weaving their network of traders and mules. On one of those trips, the couple was in Bogota. There, Griselda was made the new queen of the cocaine market and gained a name that would represent her in front of their allies and rivals and, later, the whole world.

One night in Bogota, Alberto Bravo had gone to a nightclub. Griselda had somehow suspected that Bravo was stealing from her. That was inadmissible. She had noticed that some money was going missing. She didn't know who was stealing from her, but suspected everyone, including her own husband. Even though they were married, Griselda didn't forget he was a smuggler and a criminal. She had learned to trust nobody. That night, Griselda was determined to unmask him.

Griselda went to the bar where she knew her husband was. Instead of directly confronting him, she approached his car, parked outside the club, and opened the trunk what she found inside made her furious. She found millions of dollars hidden in bags inside the car. She was driven to many conclusions. Perhaps Bravo had taken that money without her permission, thus he was stealing from her. Perhaps Bravo had earned that money from a parallel business hidden from Griselda thus, he was going to keep all that fortune for himself. Or perhaps Bravo was thinking about investing all that money—Griselda's money—without asking.

Griselda didn't take too long to decide which of the options was more likely to be true. She didn't like it either. She wouldn't tolerate her husband cheating on her, stealing from her, or even making decisions about their business together without her permission. It was her business, and she wouldn't share the lead with anyone, even her husband.

After closing violently the trunk of the car, she walked toward the club entrance. She entered, looking for her husband. When she eventually found her, she took out a weapon and pointed at him. Bravo was surrounded by his bodyguards while Griselda pointed at him. Griselda wasn't alone either; she also had her men who only obeyed her.

A shootout started between both groups. Griselda was holding a pistol while her husband used a Uzi sub-machine gun to defend himself. Everybody opened fire. Six of Bravo's bodyguards were killed, and also Bravo. Griselda herself shot him in the mouth two times to make sure she hadn't failed her shots (Turner, 2024). While she shot, she told him that nobody ever dared to touch her money or challenge her power again.

Bravo was killed. Griselda was also wounded that night. A bullet from her husband's Uzi reached her stomach. Despite the injury being serious, Griselda recovered quickly from it and was ready to assume the whole power of her new empire (Turner, 2024).

The execution of Alberto Bravo earned Griselda the name of the Black Widow. At that moment, it wasn't certain if her first husband had also been killed by her or by her men following her commands. When it was confirmed that Griselda had killed Bravo herself, the hypothesis of Trujillo's murder became possible. The motives would have been the same: Griselda wouldn't stand men putting their hands on her money. Trujillo was an obstacle for Griselda to upgrade her business from smuggling marijuana to cocaine, and Bravo was in the middle of Griselda's connection with the Medellin cartel. Both men hampered her interests and thus, she simply removed them.

The Black Widow wouldn't stop there. She would enlarge her list of killed husbands in the future. Meanwhile, her ruthlessness toward the men who shared her life was a strong proof of how far she was eager to reach to ensure her position of power.

All The Power To Griselda

In the early 1970s, Griselda Blanco passed from being a marginal character of the suburbs of New York to the master of the drug market. Moving from New York to Miami allowed her to settle in the heart of the landscape of drug dealing. Miami would soon become the capital of the drug market roads.

Even before the men around her were aware of the monster emerging, Griselda showed her skills to manage a large-scale business with innovative ideas, creative enough to evade the increasing control of the U.S. authorities. Griselda wouldn't be remembered only for the cruelty of her crimes but also for the creation of a unique smuggling technique employed even at present. The mules are still one of the most frequent ways to smuggle drugs and continue to be a preferred mechanism displayed by dealers to buy people's will and force them to work for them.

Griselda had lived all her short life on the edges of law, and danger wasn't unknown to her. It isn't a surprise that she stepped confidently into the realm of the most dangerous landlords of drug dealing. Her early connections with the Medellin cartel contributed to leave her in the center of the scene. Pablo Escobar, the Ochoa brothers, and Carlos Lehder were building the most deadly, wealthy, and profitable criminal organization. They were a significant element in Griselda's emerging empire because they provided the cocaine she eventually distributed in the U.S. market. However, Griselda managed to put them to work to her benefit and dominate them. The Medellin cartel was feared by people, drug dealers, and the Colombian government, but they all feared Griselda.

However, her rise to power wasn't complete yet. She had a solid market in Miami with connections to other parts of the country and had her supply facilities in Colombia. She had evaded the DEA and the U.S. authorities and set the stage to dominate the Medellin cartel. Yet, Griselda wanted more. In this early stage of the reign, she was still the shadow of her husband. Bravo had led the relationships with the Medellin cartel. Griselda also showed early that she wouldn't tolerate anyone who could challenge her power or treason.

The father of her child was an obstacle. He prevented Griselda from controlling everything. Moreover, he committed an unforgettable crime: He tried to fool her. Griselda had to show him and everyone around what she was capable of. So, she killed him by herself. Just like in the past, she gained the fear and respect of everyone in her neighborhood by killing that young boy they had kidnapped; she killed her own husband. It was solid evidence of who Griselda Blanco was. She would only have enough when she had it all.

With Bravo out of the scene, Griselda became the only head of the drug trade that connected the most powerful cartel in Colombia with the United States, and she had then all the power. She reached there thanks to her intelligence but even more to her ruthlessness, which only rose as she got more and more power.

CHAPTER 4
THE MIAMI CARTEL

By the late 1970s, Griselda had left Colombia. She had got rid of her husband and was the only boss. She went back to the United States and settled permanently in Miami. Dominating Florida ensured the highest power position. There, Griselda built the basis of her own cartel, the Miami cartel and soon, she found a way to fuel the rivalries between the other cartels and minor dealers to force them to work for her benefit.

Within less than five years, still in her early 20s and having killed two husbands, Griselda Blanco set up a huge and carefully arranged cocaine ring. According to records, before the decade ended, she was trafficking 3,400 pounds of cocaine a month at $50,000 a pound when it was sold in the streets (Ovalle, 2024; *The Colombian Cartels*, n.d.).

However, Griselda needed more than her entourage of couriers or Lehder's planes. She had to ensure that everyone would follow her rules. So, Griselda used two main resources: weapons to exert violence and money to subjugate people's needs. Griselda found a way to manipulate both the most vulnerable people who accepted to sell and transport the drugs for money to survive and the most powerful, from whom she collected a fee to be part of the business, but especially, she showed them the price to pay for betrayal.

As the business grew, Griselda's violence escalated to unprecedented levels. If, in the emergence of her business, she invented the mules' system, in this stage of empire, she introduced another innovative—and deadly—invention: motorcyclist hit-men. Griselda put a price on people's lives and on people's will to kill. After Griselda, the Medellin cartel used hitmen to ensure their drug-trafficking network. She was the pioneer in making death part of a business. Killing innocents and dealers became a profitable job for all those left on the other side of society.

The violence unleashed by Griselda was brutal. Anyone could fall victim to her. She ordered to get killed people who owed her, people she owed money to, or anyone who had disrespected from her own point of view. She used death and violence and her discretion, with no limits or scruples. She made alliances but needed no allies; she just used them for her convenience. A young woman took full control of a male-dominated environment and put the authorities of three countries on their knees. This is how Griselda Blanco, the Black Widow, became the Queen of Cocaine, the queen of the Miami cartel.

<u>The Empire Era</u>

An empire is characterized for being a large territorial entity that consists of multiple states or minor territories that obey a centralized supreme authority, usually ruled by a single person—the emperor. The strategies deployed by emperors to conquer and dominate territories might include direct coercion, persuasion, or indirect aggression by promoting exposure to another enemy. Eventually, any of these strategies compel the minor entity to surrender the power of the most powerful either because they can't confront it, they can obtain benefits from it, or they need protection.

Within an empire, the emperor might allow each entity to develop their own political and social ecosystem. The emperor will let each entity thrive as much as possible and, finally, gather all the profits. The elements that constitute the empire might be left to grow as much as they don't become a threat to the central power. In fact, the emperor's power can be strengthened by controlled tensions among the dominated territories. Sometimes, the emperor accepts to sacrifice the weaker segments of their domain in search of ensuring domination over the rest.

In any of those senses, Griselda Blanco was able to build an empire. Within less than ten years, Griselda Blanco put under her power most of the relevant players in the drug market. She managed to let them play their own game, evolve, and compete, only to serve her interests.

Old Competitors, New Rivals

The advance of drug production and importation to the United States wasn't limited to the Colombian cartels. Alongside the Colombian-manufactured Bolivian-Peruvian cocaine, Mexico was another major provider of drugs to the U.S. market. Due to the proximity and many flaws in the frontier, the Mexican cartels were able to smuggle significant shipments of marijuana, cocaine, and other narcotics at cheaper costs and less complex logistics, even before the rise of the Medellin cartel. During the 1970s, Mexican cartels had grown stronger.

In the 1960s and 1970s, the Sinaloa cartel emerged as one of the most powerful criminal organizations. Sinaloa is a state on the West Coast of Mexico, and it became the epicenter of the cultivation of marijuana. Also, traffickers established laboratories and manufactured heroin. Families of small, vulnerable communities in Sinaloa started smuggling marijuana to later trade it on a larger scale. Names like Pedro Avilés and Joaquín Guzmán Loera, IKA "El Chapo" became the Mexican equivalents to the Colombian drug lords (Insight Crime, 2024).

By the end of the 1970s, the Mexican dealers diversified their activities and entered the Colombian cocaine routes besides the aerial routes through the Caribbean and Norman's Kay run by Lehder, the Medellin cartel incorporated into the Guadalajara route. Guadalajara is the capital city of the state of Jalisco. Mexican dealers became active elements of the Colombian connection to introduce cocaine to the United States via air and also sea.

The Mexican branch of cocaine trading ended up working to Griselda's benefit in the middle and long term. While Avilés, El Chapo, and others could have emerged as competitors, they all turned into more pieces in Griselda's gear. The intensification of drug trading in the Mexican Gulf reinforced Griselda's position in Florida. Part of the drug was shipped to Los Angeles, and another part was sent to New York, but most of it entered through the state of Florida.

On another hand, the intricacies of the connection between the Mexican and Colombian traders made them compete against each other. At first, Griselda had put her efforts into producing her own drugs when establishing cocaine labs in Medellin. By the late 1970s, she had found a comfortable place in the supply chain as the receiver and distributor of the shipment in the United States. Thus, she was above and beyond the frictions and skirmishes among the different cartels and dealers. She needed them, but she didn't depend on a sole provider. On the contrary, they all needed her to introduce their goods effectively.

While Colombian and Mexican, and later other minor groups from other Central American countries, fought for a room in Griselda's empire, she had the power to choose one over another. In the middle and long term, the emergence of more cartels and laboratories led to open confrontation. The attacks and conspiracy among the different cartels evolved and increased during the 1980s and intensified in the early 1990s. Nonetheless, Griselda seemed to be beyond those conflicts.

Griselda didn't enjoy the monopoly of drug trading in the United States, but she did have a privileged position in Miami. When the Mexicans accessed the drugs route via Miami, Griselda was already the referent in Miami and strongly linked to the Medellin cartel. She had access to a varied range of options regarding quality and prices. Moreover, her bond with multiple providers allowed her to influence the price and down them if she wanted to. In other words, she had everything to gain from negotiation.

Unlike any of the cartels that heavily relied on Griselda's distribution network, she had nothing to fear if the DEA or the

Mexican or Colombian governments caught them. She could easily replace them with other providers.

DEA's Indirect Help

As explained before, the United States was concerned about the increasing flooding of Latin American drugs. There were other profitable markets for drug dealing, but the proximity and the established routes made the United States a preferred destination. However, the attention of the DEA during the 1970s, while the Medellin cartel and Griselda Blanco raised their empire, was driven to other drugs such as heroin and other synthetic narcotics.

In 1975, the DEA created the first specialized department with its headquarters in Washington, the Central Tactical Program (CENTAC). The main target was the major drug organizations located in Lebanon, other countries in Asia, and Mexico. Griselda was already on the DEA's list of cocaine smugglers, but the organization to fight against drugs was still incipient. The economic and logistics efforts were targeted at these other points, meaning that the Colombian connection still had an open road to escalate their activities.

Nonetheless, the DEA and the CENTAC operations were impactful enough to make Latin American drug dealers cautious. The CENTAC effectively dismantled criminal groups producing LSD, PCP, and amphetamines in Mexico, Puerto Rico, and the Dominican Republic, showcasing how far they could reach (*Drug Enforcement Administration*, n.d.). These operations were publicly displayed as a warning to criminal organizations, even though in many senses, it was used to adapt and shift the strategies.

The possibility of being caught by the DEA and being extradited to the United States became an obsession with Latin American drug lords. Thus, this external threat pushed them to rely even more on Griselda, who was in the United States and had already played under their rules.

Soon, the Latin American cartels witnessed how the DEA penetrated their countries' frontiers. In 1976, for instance, the Mexican government collaborated with the DEA in what was called Operation Trizo. The U.S. government donated helicopters that sprayed herbicides on the crops in Sinaloa, and other states engaged in drug cultivation of raw material to process heroin. About 22,000 acres of poppy were destroyed in Sinaloa, Durango, and Chihuahua, while more than 4,000 members of the Mexican cartels were arrested (*Drug Enforcement Administration*, n.d.).

The Mexican network of drug traffic was a big player on the global chessboard. Instead of becoming a threat to Griselda, she was ready to take advantage of the strikes blown by the DEA and the Mexican government. DEA had focused on heroin and other drugs, and the major targets were these producers. This caused a shift in the market that eventually turned things to Griselda's advantage.

The Shift in the Market

In the first half of the 1970s, the use of substances increased. Alongside marijuana, drug use included pharmacological drugs such as phencyclidine (PCP), amphetamines, and heroin. The problem was increasing at a fast pace. The average of deaths for PCP-related causes increased by 60% between 1976 and 1977, and 35 out of 36 deaths involved the substance that year. Moreover, the overall laboratory seizures during that period were 42% higher than the total of the two previous years (*Drug Enforcement Administration*, n.d.). It isn't coincidental that this was the major concern for DEA and Latin American governments.

In this landscape, Griselda made a risky and witty bet. She was able to read well the signs. Her resources to enter the drug market were indeed limited, but still, Griselda didn't bring her checkers to these pharmacological drugs. Instead, she observed another emerging phenomenon. She was aware of the new risks of drug trading since she was compelled to leave the United States to avoid getting caught. Nonetheless, her sense of smell for market gaps allowed her to recognize the potential of other drugs that were gaining the streets: marijuana and cocaine.

Indeed, in the middle and late 1970s, the drug market shifted from lab-made drugs to Colombian marijuana and cocaine. According to records, the seizure of a 100-pound shipment of cocaine became a usual procedure (*Drug Enforcement Administration*, n.d.). Griselda gained perspective of this new gap while she traveled between Medellin and Miami until she definitely settled in the strategic city of the peninsula.

The harbors and landing strips were already settled in Florida. They were used to receive maritime vessels, small yachts, and go-fast boats in all sizes of Colombian Gold (marijuana) shipments. By the early 1980s, the DEA had conducted several operations to halt the arrival of drugs to the United States. Again, Griselda's strategy was directed to that element that was out of scope. If authorities searched dealers who smuggled pharmaceutical drugs and marijuana, she focused on the drug that was spreading on the streets and nightclubs.

Cocaine, the "Benign" Drug

Griselda was favored by another contextual element. Marijuana is considered a major problem in the United States regarding substance abuse because of the high reach of its consumption. It was out of control and the success of the business was making the dealers too stronger. Drugs, as President Nixon had said, were the new public enemy, and the gangs' powers were increasing violence and death in the bigger cities.

The other main target was pharmaceutical drugs. Cocaine wasn't on the list of the most dangerous drugs. It would be inexact to affirm that the DEA didn't take care of cocaine trading. However, cocaine was considered a less dangerous drug if compared to the others. In the early 1970s, the U.S. laws misidentified cocaine as a "narcotic," meaning it was produced for medical purposes, and the Comprehensive Drug Abuse Prevention and Control Act defined it as "'Schedule II:' having medical use and a high abuse potential" (Drake & Scott, 2019, para. 9).

Many experts point out that the demonization and fierce persecution of amphetamines eventually drove people to cocaine, increasing its popularity (Drake & Scott, 2019). The statistics of the decade regarding cocaine abuse are outstanding. Surveys convey that by 1974, 5.4 million U.S. citizens admitted having tried cocaine at least once. Only five years later, new surveys revealed that at least 20% of the population had used cocaine in the last year, and 9.3%

had consumed it in the last month (*Drug Enforcement Administration*, n.d.).

Despite these records, people and authorities saw cocaine merely as a recreational drug and was depicted in the media as a benign substance celebrated for its "pleasurability." On one occasion, Dr. Peter Bourne, President Jimmy Carter's drug advisor, made a public declaration (Drug Enforcement Administration, n.d.) stating that:

Cocaine...is probably the most benign of illicit drugs currently in widespread use. At least as strong a case could be made for legalizing it as for legalizing marijuana. Short-acting...not physically addicting, and acutely pleasurable, cocaine has found increasing favor at all socioeconomic levels (p. 45).

The relaxed attitude of the authorities and extended popular acceptance made cocaine a substance at the reach of people of all walks. A National Survey on Drug Abuse reported in 1979 that two-thirds of young adults had experienced cocaine or marijuana, and about 3 out of 10 children and teens between 12 and 17 years old had used cocaine at least once.

The market was quickly expanding, and the problem was quickly rising. For Griselda, it was the perfect landscape to build her empire. Nonetheless, the counterpart for that was a new approach to cocaine from the authorities. Eventually, that would raise the risks for the business. Griselda didn't fear back from challenges and was used to playing on the limits, so for her, these were unparalleled opportunities to sit at the top of the drug market pyramid.

Miami, Griselda's Kingdom

To briefly recap, the DEA and authorities had focused on the Mexican drug smuggling of pharmaceutical drugs and marijuana. The U.S. society had driven away from these drugs and had exponentially increased the levels of cocaine abuse. Florida was on the DEA drug map and many operations were carried out there, but still, the peninsula became the drug capital of the Western hemisphere, particularly Miami, Griselda's home (*Drug Enforcement Administration*, n.d.).

According to official sources, Miami wasn't only attractive for its matchless geographical position but also for the large net of cooperative international banks. Before the 1970s decade ended, South Florida was crowded with Latin American cocaine traffickers, and Griselda was boss of most of them.

Griselda Blanco consolidated her empire between 1975 and 1979. Records of that time reveal that in 1975, the U.S. Customs Service gathered 729 pounds of cocaine, and cocaine loads intercepted in Miami airport passed from 37 to 271 pounds. In 1979, cocaine trading became the biggest industry in the city. Miami, on other days, a peaceful beach and tourist attraction, was the capital of drugs, with revenues that reached $10 billion a year. Administrator Bensinger once claimed that there was so much money that instead of counting it, dealers weighed it (*Drug Enforcement Administration*, n.d.).

In the early 1980s, the Miami cartel and its Colombian and Mexican providers traded 125 tons of cocaine. A kilo of pure cocaine was sold for $800,000. Nonetheless, that was just the beginning. Within the next few years, the price of cocaine dropped because the offer drastically increased. For instance, it is known that in 1984, one kilo of pure cocaine was sold at $30,000 in New York and $16,000 in South Florida (*Drug Enforcement Administration*, n.d.).

No matter how many providers accessed South Florida's market to attend to an ever-expanding demand, Griselda had control of the business. She was at the top, and the center of the whole net, and that allowed her to amass a formidable fortune. However, the drug trade was a violent terrain, and Griselda needed more than just money and managerial abilities to hold on to her enterprise.

The Drug Wars

The drug wars have two sides. On one of those sides, there was the DEA and the different countries' governments joining efforts to dismantle the criminal network. The miscalculation of cocaine's impact on society caused a severe delay in the authorities' accurate reaction to restrain the spread of cocaine trading. At first, the cocaine network went unnoticed, but soon, the DEA started connecting the dots. Each shipment seized in the airport or from boats and ships wasn't an isolated case. Over time, the DEA realized that they were all part of a unified network.

The monopoly of cocaine smuggling was in the Colombian cartel's hands. While Manhattan and Queens in New York were hot spots, the major center of the network had its base in Miami. Progressively, the DEA became one of Griselda's greatest enemies because, as she ascended as the cocaine queen, she also became a main target for the organization.

DEA found out that the Miami cartel processed 70% of the total of the cocaine that entered the United States. That is a strong monopoly on the market. That meant over $150 million in profits a year for the dealers. Griselda's net included the already well-known Medellin cartel, the Guadalajara route, and some Cuban dealers that also introduced their drug loads via Miami. Eventually, Griselda attracted them and made them enter her empire.

Despite the DEA having clues about the huge network working underground, the organization struggled to spot the face at the top of the organization. They knew Griselda, and they were after her, but still, the DEA didn't connect such a well-designed and sophisticated smuggling and trading mechanism. Some experts claim the DEA never expected a woman on top of such an organization.

DEA dealt with limitations to uncover the fabric of the Miami cartel, but meanwhile, it devoted many efforts to increasing its capacity to fight the war on drugs. Between 1975 and 1979, the DEA increased the training time for its students and continued to acquire the latest technology to track information. For instance, the DEA employed the Policefax DD-14. This was a fax machine that allowed them to transmit information about the criminals, for instance, fingerprints. The Central Identification Bureau transmitted information about the suspects, shortening the time to properly identify and arrest them. However, the machine took many hours to transmit the images, and these still lacked high definition, hampering the possibilities to use them effectively.

The government raised the guard, and Griselda confronted a progressively stronger enemy. However, time would prove that she had learned how to evade them. She had many other threats to deal with. It wasn't an easy task to have the most dangerous drug dealers in the world under control. In that, she also succeeded.

That was, in fact, the other side of the drug wars: the war unleashed among the different cartels and minor groups. They fought over territory, money, harbors, landing strips, and market shares. Griselda developed a thorough system to keep them off. Nobody within her network would disobey her rules or take her money.

Griselda had an empire to rule, and that meant that she didn't only deal with her people. Violence and confrontation had reached every corner of the city. Drug trading had permeated society, reaching unprecedented levels, and Griselda also discovered how to use that to her benefit. She found prospective dealers and allies everywhere, and she knew how to engage them in her mesh.

New Allies and Subjects

Griselda Blanco settled in Miami and built her empire, the Miami cartel. Besides her close connections with the Medellin cartel and the Mexican cartels, she established complex connections with other dealers that operated in Florida. Griselda managed to deal with competitors and bring them under their ring of power to make them either her allies or her victims.

In fact, Griselda didn't owe loyalty to any of them. She approached them to grab their share in the market, compel them to obey her, and use them to her benefit. Florida was a center for drug dealers, and by the late 1970s, dealers from Mexico, Cuba, Puerto Rico, and other Latin American countries had come to build their own drug trading networks.

The Falcon brothers were two Cuban drug kingpins who settled in Florida. Augusto Guillermo "Willy" Falcon was the most powerful of the duo. He had reached Florida around 1978 and started selling drugs he obtained from the same providers as Griselda, the Medellin cartel. His brother, Gustavo "Taby" Falcon, also joined the business and during the 1980s, he was also involved in the war wars. They were responsible for dozens of murders that flooded Florida's streets with blood and violence.

Willy Falcon teamed up with his schoolmate, Salvador "Sal" Magluta, also from Cuba. Together, they gained popularity as the most prolific Caribbean drug smugglers. They were known as "Los Muchachos" (the guys, in Spanish). They met when they were teenagers and attended the same elementary school. Soon, they left school and dedicated themselves to raising their own criminal organization.

Los Muchachos established connections with Escobar, Lehder, and Blanco and became important links in the supply chain. They were masters in controlling speedboats. Therefore, they were in charge of driving cocaine from the Bahamas and other shore strategic locations and taking them to Florida. There, they delivered the shipment to Griselda and other distributors. According to records, Falcon and Magluta smuggled 68 tons of cocaine into the state of Florida (den Held & Voss, 2023).

Later, Los Muchachos didn't only perform as transporters. They fully engaged in the drug wars and were known as the Cocaine Cowboys, along with other dealers, also below Griselda's influence. They started as small drug dealers and reached the top of the business, hand in hand with Blanco. They paid the cost of killing and risking their lives to serve Queen Griselda. Simultaneously, they became popular speedboat racers, using their abilities for sport as well as for smuggling. Their popularity served them to cover their criminal records for years and evade police persecution.

Another relevant player in Griselda's game was Mickey Munday. He was from Miami and an early associate of the Medellin cartel. He entered the smuggling business almost by accident. He found a large load of marijuana in a dead friend's house. He sold the drug and made a small fortune. With the money, he bought a 680 Aero Commander, his first plane, which he used to smuggle cocaine from Colombia.

Munday entered the Colombian-Miami connection and, thus, became part of Griselda's network. According to his own testimonial, he and his partner, Jon Roberts, smuggled 300 to 500 kilos a trip every two to three days (Elguera, 2023). Being a former pilot, he became a strategic piece to delivering cocaine but also engaged in the raid of violence unleashed by Griselda and the other dealers.

Another relevant pilot was Barry Seal. Born Adler Berriman Seal, he was interested in planes from an early age. That youth interest ended up as the springboard to becoming another link in the Colombian cocaine route. He acted like a double agent. He first entered the Civil Air Patrol (CAP) in Baton Rouge, though he also sold weapons to Cuban rebels. Later, he would also work for the CIA but was closely engaged with the Medellin cartel.

Seal entered the business in 1975 but was arrested in 1979 in Honduras, where he arrived with 40 kilos of cocaine. While he was in prison, he met one of the Ochoa brothers' men, William Roger Reeves. That meant Seal's entrance into the drug business. By the 1980s, the Medellin cartel was something more than just a drug trading network. They became a complex criminal organization.

Plata o Plomo

Drug dealing didn't work as any licit business. The trading net was complex and required many people and an exhaustive logistic organization. The amounts of drugs and money were enormous. Besides delivering, storing, and selling the drugs on the streets and to minor distributors, the organization required close control to avoid any of the components from deviating from the expected steps and routes. In other words, Griselda needed a lot of people to carry on her business and many others to keep them under control.

Griselda deployed two main strategies to recruit people for her organization based on a popular and tragic motto, "*plata o plomo*"— money or plumb, meaning pay or die. Money was essential to provide people with weapons and ensure transportation. The leaders of the cartels collected funds from the lower levels of the organization. For instance, the Ochoa brothers claimed for the Medellin cartel $7 billion dollars a year from each cocaine family engaged in their network. Griselda also asked for a substantial commission from the dealers who depended on her to distribute the drugs on Miami streets.

Griselda used the money to support the logistics of her organization but also to recruit people, buy their loyalty either to her, or persuade enemies to work for her. Griselda also employed money for extortion or bribery. She paid policemen, officers, investigators, and other authorities to avoid being persecuted and covered for her criminal activities. This explains, in part, why Griselda and most of the other cartel members were able to carry on their activities for so long without being caught.

Hitmen and Motorcycles

Besides money, the other key resource Griselda relied on was violence. She inaugurated a new form of organized violence: motorcycle hitmen. She recruited men to join her personal army. They were trained to kill, and Griselda paid them to engage in violent raids to kill whoever Griselda wanted to get rid of. She had already paid men to kill her first husband (according to some of the versions as explained before), but over time, she made it a key element of her criminal organization. In fact, she proudly credited herself for creating this unique type of hitman: men using motorbikes to lurk, persecute, and execute victims in any place, at any moment.

Griselda had no issues finding an available workforce for her criminal organization. Hundreds of people were eager to join her ranks. The job implied killing people, most of the time criminals, but also missions implied killing innocents. Hitmen were at risk of being caught and sent to prison, killed during their raids, or discharged by the boss, Griselda, because they knew too much or were too dangerous for her. She had killed her own husband because she distrusted him; she would trust no one.

Despite all these risks, Griselda didn't struggle to recruit hitmen. She used her money and knowledge of the lowest levels of society and recruited his personal soldiers among illegal immigrants, many of them Cuban, like the Falcon brothers and Magluta, who served as relevant connections. Florida was also a preferred place for immigrants coming from Cuba because of its geographical location. In the 1960s and 1970s, many Cubans fled from their country after the triumph of Castro's revolution in 1959. They reached Florida, sailing across the sea on precarious boats and rafts. They came to the United States with nothing and, thus, nothing to lose. This made them an easy prey for Griselda.

The Notorious Right-Hand Hitman

Even though Griselda didn't trust anyone around her, one of her hitmen became her righthand man. His name was Jorge "Rivi" Ayala. His nickname was Riverita, and he took it from a Colombian cartoon due to his high-pitched voice.

He was born in Colombia but lived almost all of his life in the United States. He grew up in Chicago and started his life outside the law, smuggling illegal immigrants. By 1979, he took another step. He started transporting weapons from Chicago to Miami, and there, he found many opportunities to expand his criminal activities.

He started working as a debt collector. His methods to persuade debtors included torture, extortion, and, eventually, death. That is how Griselda met him and took him into her personal army. She was cruel, even more than Ayala, but he decided to serve her. She respected him and valued his talent to execute his job with no complaints and no mistakes. Both qualities were priceless to Griselda.

It is believed that Ayala committed over 250 crimes commissioned by Griselda. She would appoint him the most relevant missions to be certain there would be no flaws. One of the crimes was against Alfredo and Grizel Lorenzo. Griselda ordered Rivi to kill them because they hadn't paid for a cocaine shipment. He shot them in cold blood while the couple's children were watching TV in the next room.

The star hitman was also in charge of getting rid of one of the Miami cartel's former members, Jesus "Chucho" Castro. Rivi gathered a team and opened fire in Castro's car. On that occasion, Rivi failed the mission. Castro survived the attack. Nonetheless, Griselda was still pleased with Rivi because the shooting killed Castro's two-year-old son, and that was enough to make Griselda pleased.

Ayala worked for Griselda for several years and was her deadliest hitman. However, he wouldn't remain loyal until the end.

Make Way for the Queen

During the 1970s and in the early 1980s, Blanco consolidated her position as one of the most powerful masters in the world's drug market capital, Florida. As her power increased, so did violence. Amidst the chaos, Blanco became the Cocaine Godmother.

The context had dramatically changed. Cocaine wasn't only a symbol of status or privately destined for celebrities; eventually, cocaine reached and flooded the streets of the United States. This only increased the opportunities to keep expanding the business.

The Medellin cartel consolidated its position, ensuring the routes via the Bahamas. The drug was transported from the Colombian laboratories through the Caribbean and later through the Panama connection. However, they weren't the only ones. Other cartels emerged and became fierce competitors, not only in Colombia but also in Mexico and even in the United States. Griselda had to adapt to this new context and navigate rivalries, sometimes exploiting them to her benefit. Eventually, she managed to recruit all the dealers that she could, forcing them to betray each other. The criminal organizations were divided, and that led to an escalation of violence in what was known as the drug wars.

On the other side, the war on drugs is also exacerbated. As Griselda's power increased and the Medellin cartel smuggled more and more amounts of cocaine, the DEA and the United States doubled the efforts to stop the inflow of cocaine. However, the hunt for the great drug lords would take a long to make them withdraw. For years, Griselda and the other cartels had time and freedom to spread the market and amass fortune.

Griselda became the female depiction of the mafia, as portrayed in Francis Ford Coppola's *The Godfather* released in 1972. She was the real she-name of the mafia, and she would make use of and abuse such power.

CHAPTER 5
THE "COCAINE COWBOYS"

Many times in history, societies were dragged into an escalation of violence that reached inexplicable levels. It doesn't happen overnight, but at some point, violent episodes that used to happen every time to time become the headlines of the newspapers and prime-time TV shows almost daily. Suddenly, issues that initially seemed to be only some marginal groups' problems become everyone's threat. One day, nobody feels safe walking around the streets or quietly shopping in a mall.

It isn't like violent groups emerged out of nowhere and decided to go out and shoot anyone. The handwriting was on the wall, but nobody seemed to see it. Dealers and hitmen had been there for a long time, and the authorities were aware of them, but they were supposed to remain underground, tangled up in their murky businesses, and kill each other. Drugs weren't breaking down news in the United States by the early 1980s. They were openly sold in the streets, and while the government had tried to control the entrance of drugs into the country, they were aware of the large criminal bands that evolved thanks to a rising and profitable business. It was evident that they had their "*plata o plomo*" way of functioning, but it was not supposed to reach the rest of society.

In the 1930s, a war was unleashed among the organized crime gangs and between them and the authorities. Common people were supposed to be left aside from the conflict. Criminals only dealt with criminals, and the authorities had the resources to persecute them with no collateral damage. It failed once, and it would fail again. Griselda Blanco, as the leader of the Miami cartel, didn't care how far she had to go to strengthen her power and expand her business. She even relied on widespread panic to show drug dealers and common people which was the right side to be on: hers.

Griselda inaugurated a new era of out-of-control violence anywhere and for no certain reason. She targeted her rivals but also used innocent casualties to press on the government. She used open, public, and explicit violence to persuade people that it was best to do what Griselda said. Griselda could offer protection, help take revenge, offer "job and good money" opportunities, and a place in a chaotic system that pushed them away. Still, the price to pay was too high, and not everyone had the chance to choose.

The Shootout at the Local Mall

It was a Wednesday afternoon, and the streets and shops of Miami were bustling with people despite the heat. It was July 11, 1979, and none of the people who gathered in the nearby area of the Crown Liquors shop could ever imagine what they were going to witness.

The Crown Liquors was a typically crowded place on the west end of the Deadland Mall in South Florida. At around 2:30 in the afternoon, people shopping and having a drink there were taken by surprise when two Latin men entered, carrying firearms. After them, a group of three other Latin males also entered. Some witnesses affirmed that they were more. Once inside, the armed men opened fire without previous warning.

The target was a well-known drug dealer, a member of a Colombian drug trafficking network named German Jimenez Panesso, and his bodyguard, Juan Carlos Hernandez. Both men were inside the store, and when the others opened fire, they responded, leading to a crossfire with the rest of the people still inside the building.

The result of the shooting was that two people died at the scene; neither of them was a member of any gang. One of the victims was a 21-year-old man named Alfredo J. Milian and a 25-year-old woman named Odalys Espinosa. According to records, three other people were injured during the shooting and had to be hospitalized due to severe bullet wounds. The episode was later known as the Dadeland Mall Massacre and is remembered as one of the boldest attacks on public places perpetrated by gangs linked to drug dealing.

After the shooting, the aggressor, who had entered the store, ran away in a van that had a scripture on the sides. It was labeled "Happy Time Completely Party Supply." The van was abandoned at the far end of the parking lot of the mall. Shortly after, the police found it and could easily recognized due to the scripture on the sides. It was confirmed that the perpetrators of the attack were the so-called Cocaine Cowboys, Griselda Blanco's personal army.

The police who had arrived at the place engaged in persecution, but there was nothing they could do. Later, the police officer explained that the lawmen were outgunned. The police affirmed that the van was a "war wagon" with MAC-10s, carabins, pistols, and shotguns. A police officer said, "That was a stark realization of how outgunned we were because back then, the only weapon we were allowed to carry was a six-shot .38-caliber revolver" (Richardson, 2024, para. 26-27).

The Dadeland Mall Massacre served as a public presentation of the Cocaine Cowboys and the Miami cartel, though people didn't know yet that Griselda Blanco was behind the curtain. It was also a call for attention and a warning to the authorities and society. The hitmen weren't wearing masks, used an easily recognizable vehicle, and left it abandoned with weapons and proof that led to who they were. They weren't hiding, and they weren't concerned about being recognized. On the contrary, they wanted everybody to know who had struck at daylight and got their way.

Officer Andreu was at the place and said (Hamacher, 2019):

These guys will go out there, and if they want to hit or kill someone, it doesn't matter where it happens, who else is around, or the time of day that it happens; they're gonna get their target, and everyone else better be careful and be aware of their surroundings (para. 8).

It didn't take long for the authorities to connect the dots and follow the trace left by the Cocaine Cowboys. Until then, Griselda Blanco was a marginal name. After the Dadeland Mall Massacre, Griselda became the main public enemy: "The Dadeland shooting was the first time Al Singleton, a retired homicide detective, had heard of Blanco. The Miami PD received knowledge from the DEA that Blanco may have been involved" (Richardson, 2024, para. 26).

Griselda wasn't concerned. She was ready for the main stage. She had raised an empire and had an army of motorcycle hitmen who worked for her. She had money and resources to make the world feel her power and fear her. If the system had decided to chase her, she wouldn't hide. On the contrary, her goal would be to stay always on the front. She was determined to always strike first.

The Deadland Mall Massacre was just the first move in her new criminal style. She would instill fear not only among her enemies but society. She would make everyone believe they could only be safe and keep their lives if she wanted to. The more the DEA approached, the harder her next aggression.

It is interesting to reflect on how society manages violence and crime. It is like society has a double dimension: in one of them, normal life flows, people go to work, children attend school, and enjoy their spare time throwing parties or sitting in a coffee shop with a pancake. On the other hand, violence and crime take control, and people kill and die as if the rest of the system were not even aware of it.

Throughout history, criminal organizations have evolved in the shadows, and for a long time, they kept their business and their skirmishes among themselves. However, on certain occasions, violence crosses the imaginary line that separates these dimensions, and this dark underworld seems to take the streets.

Then, it doesn't matter any longer if people are involved or not with the gangs, if they owe them money, or if they have nothing to lose and are willing to risk their lives to take others. The difference between death and life becomes just a matter of fate, of being in the wrong place at the wrong moment. In the blink of an eye, anyone innocent or guilty becomes a number of the statistics that are engrossed by violent crimes that start happening anywhere and at any time.

In the 1960s and 1970s, drugs flooded the streets of the main cities in the United States, and dealers engaged in commissioned crime with specific targets, always related to drug dealing. The reasons were betrayal, stealing, or fighting over marketplace niches. Certainly, drugs reached all levels of society, but the scope of violence was somewhat limited to their own underground world, aside from the law and ruled by their own sense of justice and order. The legal system didn't overlook the increasing violence and described the government's displayed resources to stop, or at least control, organized crime. Yet, they failed. On the contrary, as the government increased the pressure on the criminal organizations, they developed adaptive strategies to regain strength.

These adaptive strategies, far from pushing crime back and forcing criminal organizations to hide, implied the spreading of violence to society. It became a trial of power between the drug cartels and the authorities, and in the middle, people. The shootout at the mall at daylight, ordered by Griselda Blanco, shifted the course of the war. It was no longer a war on drugs or a war among cartels; it became a war against society and its basic rules.

It was the beginning of a new mean of consolidating and showcasing power that other cartels later emulated. The use of terror used common people as bargaining chips in their resistance and attack against the state forces. Griselda would not spare blood and death to prove how far she was willing to reach to hold her position.

The Cocaine Cowboys Reach the Headlines

By 1979, the Miami drug cartel was consolidated, and the DEA was aware of that. The authorities weren't taken completely by surprise when Griselda's men perpetrated the attack in the mall. However, the modus operandi, the size, and lethality of the weapons were a new element to consider. The criminals displayed an unprecedented recklessness that depicted a new type of enemy. They were conveying a powerful and cynical message of how violence would be played in public places, and that shifted the DEA and government's strategy to fight against organized crime and its head, Griselda Blanco.

The men who entered the Crown Liquors shop weren't the Cocaine Cowboys themselves. They were just hitmen hired to kill. The real Cocaine Cowboys were Willy Falcon and Salvador "Sal" Magluta, characters that were introduced in Chapter 4. These young Cuban immigrants were well-known in the Miami immigrant community. They had started smuggling marijuana and then shifted to cocaine, adapting to the new trends in the business.

Willy Falcon and Sal Magluta became Griselda's traders and were responsible for bringing the loads of cocaine into the United States. Los Muchachos, as they were known, were popular because they were boat racers. They displayed an eccentric life of luxury and excess that they could never explain. However, they were able to evade justice for years, even after being captured. They couldn't explain how they had made their fortune without having worked in their lives, but justice couldn't prove their crimes either. Thus, they were imprisoned only to be quickly released.

Los Muchachos, or the Cocaine Cowboys, were the backbone of Griselda's trading network and also of her personal army. They were the head, but they didn't work alone. Other relevant Cocaine Cowboys were Gustavo Falcon, Willy's brother, and Jorge Valdez, one of the organization's leaders. In the second level, Pedro Rosello and Ralph Linero were other relevant names. Linero was the driver of Willy and Sal's boat. All of them were eventually imprisoned, but with minor sentences or for other crimes.

In the 1980s, the Cocaine Cowboys also adopted another name. As Griselda Blanco's personal guard, they were known as the "Pistoleros" (shooters). Griselda used them to fight the Cocaine Cowboy Wars. She was determined to eliminate the competence and anyone who stood in her way. The shootout at the mall may have been a declaration of war.

After that day, the war unfolded, and the bodies were counted by dozens. The crimes were never solved, but they were attributed to Griselda's Cowboys because they followed similar patterns. Alongside the motorcycle hitmen, Griselda ordered the *Pistoleros* to carry out countless hits using vans like the one abandoned after the shooting. These vans were "war wagons, heavily armored with gun ports cut into the sides (Ponti, 2024). They became a real death machine.

Griselda didn't stint bullets and blood. She would kill "just in case." Instead of finding out about their victims and confirming if they were who she thought they were or if they were guilty of what she believed, she ordered the murder first. She would kill and later ask. Death became a vice, and the more she ordered and committed, the cruelest they were. Besides directly shooting people, she ordered the to leave the bodies at the side of the roads. Over time, she also ordered her men to decapitate the victims or cut them into pieces. The purpose wasn't to cover the footprints from the police; it was just to quench her thirst for death.

The Impact on Society

Despite Griselda's original objective for the attack, it had a groundbreaking impact on society. The shootout may have just been Griselda's attempt to get rid of some competitors who didn't want to enter her ring of power. Perhaps it was just a settling of scores or a warning to other potential enemies. Ultimately, it became the public presentation of Griselda's personal army, which was known to the people as the Cocaine Cowboys.

The media brought the name to the headlines not only in Florida but all over the country. The media labeled the aggressors as the Cocaine Cowboys, giving them a name and a place in public discussions. The image of the cowboy isn't coincidental. The cowboy is a familiar image in the American collective imagination. The cowboy depicts the intrepid spirit of those who dared cross the border of civilization trying to make a fortune. The cowboys were beyond the limits of law because they lived beyond the margins of the state. They were only ruled by what dictates survival.

The image of the cowboys in the Wild West, facing extreme dangers and relying only on their own strength to survive, somehow blurs the borders of what is good or wrong. Epic figures of the Old West are heroes or outlaws, depending on the perspective. When the press labeled the hitmen as cowboys, this name gave them a diminished depiction as criminals. They fought their own wars, they killed criminals like them, and they lived in a parallel world where the law didn't reach them. They created their own environment of violence.

From a present perspective, this was a mistaken approach. Violence flooded society, and anyone could fall victim to organized crime. The Dadeland Mall Massacre wasn't an isolated incident, and the casualties there weren't mere ill-fated people. It was the prelude of a new chapter of street crime, as the country had known in times of the Prohibition era when the Mafia families ruled.

However, the idea of the cowboy resonated with the audience. The public figures of people like Griselda Blanco, despite the cruelty of her acts, were controversial. The audience acknowledged their ability to overcome poverty and marginality and become powerful, wealthy businesspeople. Griselda was an illegal immigrant who reached the United States after the American dream. Instead, she had to seek other means barely to survive. Eventually, her determination and skills took her to power, and she was killed to avoid being killed. That put her—and other drug landlords—in a place where the logic of law and order was useless. Some of them were seen almost like Robin Hood, finding the gap in the system to thrive despite the odds and offering opportunities to others, even though those opportunities were based on smuggling, stealing, and killing. For those at the margins of society with nothing to lose, these were just part of their daily script.

Eventually, what might have started as an isolated event became the origin of a massive spread of panic. Griselda gained power. Raising her public profile indeed drove more looks on her, but it didn't threaten her. If she felt the police or the DEA was too close, she only needed to release a stream of street violence to remind everyone what she was capable of. Like an animal that attacks when it feels in danger, Griselda used her Cocaine Cowboys to always strike first.

In the short and middle term, the Cocaine Cowboys in the media had three main impacts on the public. The great majority felt terrorized, and the trust in the government's capacity to protect them was at risk. The government knew this, and thus, the efforts were redoubled to ensure their authority, if not on organized crime, at least in front of the eyes of the citizens.

A minor group of the audience felt compelled to collaborate with the authorities. Everybody wanted to be safe, but performing as witnesses in the cases against the Cocaine Cowboys was perhaps even greater risk than having them in the streets. When the Cocaine Cowboys were captured and taken on trial, the defense used the list of witnesses published by the prosecution. They placed advertisements in the media offering a reward to anyone who provided information about the witness. The result was that a lot of people cooperated, either moved by an economic interest or because they preferred to be considered the Cocaine Cowboys' allies. The witnesses were killed or forced to remain silent.

A significant part of the audience didn't take sides against the Cocaine Cowboys or Griselda. Many of them found them as their escape gate from poverty, while others sought protection from other gangs and also from the police. This was one of Griselda's most effective strategies: she offered opportunities to "thrive"—easy and quick money—and protection. Neither of them was available to these people in the legal realm.

Moreover, the rocketing journey of Griselda from the suburbs of Colombia to being the queen of Florida made her a heroine. The spread of voice about the Cocaine Cowboys contributed to bringing more people who wanted to work for her. It wasn't only until they were captured that her power started to decline.

The U.S. authorities intensified the fight against drugs, not only by confronting organized crime in the streets and trying to get them in their dens but also by appealing to citizens. In the mid-1980s, the *Just Say No* campaign was launched. Public figures like Nancy Reagan and Clint Eastwood aimed to persuade people, especially the youth, to reject substances. Nonetheless, the impact was diametrically opposed. The demand for cocaine and other drugs led to an expansion of the market. Eventually, the efforts to combat drugs served as free advertising for the Cocaine Cowboys and their boss, Griselda Blanco, who was there to take advantage (Bravo, 2021).

The Third Husband

The Dadeland Mall Massacre introduced Griselda Blanco to society and added her name to the DEA's list of most wanted criminals. She became a synonym for many expressions that referred to her role as the head of the major drug cartel in the United States. Nonetheless, she already had a nickname that depicted her unscrupulous nature. She was known as the Black Widow. By the end of the 1970s, she had already buried two ex-husbands.

There were some doubts about Trujillo's death, but she was the confirmed murderer of her second husband, Alberto Bravo. Another dead would enlarge the list of her victims.

Griselda met him in 1978. It wasn't an ordinary date. There are no official records, but witnesses reported that Griselda had arranged a meeting with him to hire him as one of her hitmen. His name was Dario Sepúlveda, a Colombian immigrant who was settled in Florida. He was a bank robber but also had his own criminal record. His profile fits with Griselda's requirements, but instead of hiring him to join the Cowboys, she married him.

Shortly after they got married, they settled together in Miami and had a son. Griselda's third marriage was violent and signed by death. Even though she was at the peak of her career, she was a proud woman and couldn't stand the idea of betrayal. She was very jealous of any woman around Sepúlveda. On one occasion, she gave the order to kill eight strippers because she was suspicious of them. She believed the women had slept with Sepúlveda, and as usual, she got them killed, and then she'd seek confirmation.

It was never a happy couple. Besides Griselda's jealousy and her murky business, they had many disagreements regarding their family, particularly their son. Sepúlveda wanted to send the child to school and have a normal life. Instead, Griselda didn't want the child to be outside. She was obsessed with the child's security and didn't want to risk him. That implied having him always close to her, where she could control everything around him.

In 1983, Griselda and Sepúlveda ended their marriage, and, just like the others, it was troubled. After the separation, Sepúlveda left Miami and returned to Medellin. His great mistake was to take his son with him without Griselda's permission. She would never forget that.

The versions of what truly happened then are diverse, and neither of them has been sufficiently proven. It is known that Griselda persecuted Sepúlveda in Colombia, and he ended up dead. Some sources affirm she appointed two of her hitmen to execute him, while others indicate that she was there at the moment of the murder. Regardless of where she was when Sepúlveda was killed, it is certain that Griselda was involved. However, she was never charged with her husband's crimes.

That day, Sepúlveda was driving his car. His 5-year-old son was sitting in the back seat. Sepúlveda didn't know that he was heading to Griselda's people, who had ambushed him. In the middle of the road, two men dressed like cops intercepted the car and made signals ordering him to pull over. Sepúlveda did what they told him, and the two men walked toward him. They told Sepúlveda to open the car door, and when he did so, they shot him in front of his son. The two men weren't policemen; instead, they were probably Griselda's hitmen. The Black Widow had added one more victim to her list.

The Name of the Mafia

Her son's name was Michael Corleone. Griselda didn't choose her son's name coincidentally. It was Griselda's way to refer herself as a mafia boss. Michael Corleone, played by Al Pacino, was the Godfather, Vito Corleone's son in Francis Ford Coppola's popular movie inspired by the mafia families in the United States. The Corleone were the fictional characters who depicted the mobsters that raised an empire from organized crime.

The first film of The Godfather was released in 1972, and the second, in which Michael Corleone became the head of the family, in 1974. The films were as popular as controversial. Even though the story wasn't based on real facts, it depicted the Five Families (criminal organizations) that ruled New York and contributed to spreading an ambiguous image of the gangsters. The "Godfather" was a cold-blood murder but also provided protection and rewarded loyalty. Mafia reached the sectors of society where the law and the state didn't and built a unique sense of justice. For public opinion, gangsters could be both dangerous criminals who attempted against social peace or bandit heroes who fought in the margins of society.

The image of the Cocaine Cowboys coincided with this controversial depiction of the criminal. Griselda, as the leader of the Cocaine Cowboys, accepted to play the game and assumed the role of the female counterpart of the Godfather. Then, besides being the Black Widow, she became the Cocaine Godmother.

New Name for the Queen—the Cocaine Godmother

The Godfather had a message for society: "Just as he (Michael Corleone) presides over his world, we are masters of our dream, and it is a Corleone-like axiom that we can have anything we want—if we want it enough" (Thomson, 2021, para. 1). If that was the true meaning behind the fictional character of the Godfather, then Griselda was truly the Godmother—the cocaine Godmother. She was the embodiment of will and lack of scruples to achieve her goals. The only moral principle she used to measure her acts was how much she benefited from them.

By the end of the 1970s, Griselda was, in many ways, the cocaine Godmother. She had become a powerful woman with control over the most important drug routes in the United States. The Latin American dealers from the Caribbean needed her permission to operate and introduce their drug loads, and she led an army of hitmen ready to kill anyone as she ordered it. However, Griselda didn't only enjoy the power of allowing to live or kill others. Besides being a deadly ruler of that dark kingdom, she had become a magnate.

Just like the Corlones in the film, Griselda used all her power to be as rich as she wanted. She ensured to have anything she wanted, but she did not only "want it enough;" she just took it. Her power and fortune allowed her to buy things and wills. She was one of the world's richest and most feared people. In the early 1980s, she trafficked 1.5 tons of cocaine monthly and sold it within her network in Florida and other important cities for tens of millions of dollars (Rufo, 2024). Her fortune was incalculable, and she lived a life of a celebrity.

How much she owed and how many properties and goods she had, it was never confirmed. It is known that she bought several properties in Colombia and the United States, and a mansion in Miami, which was famous not only for the luxury but for the atrocities that happened there. According to reports (Spencer-Elliott, 2024):

At least 20 other properties owned by Griselda have been found in registry office documents in Bogota and Cartagena. However, authorities estimate she could have as many as 200 houses in

Colombia, including farms in Uraba and estates in Medellin, Bello, Envigado, and San Cristobal (para. 6).

Despite Griselda's aim to keep away the DEA's target, she appeared as the owner of many of the properties, and also, she also paid mortgages on several of them. These documents were evidence of a fortune she would never be able to prove, but Griselda didn't care.

The mansion was in the heart of Miami-Dade County on the coast, surrounded by a line of islands between the Atlantic Ocean and Key Biscayne. According to the police records, the mansion was her hideout, and the location was strategic. There, she would take people to the parties she threw with no control. The drug landlords, including the infamous Pablo Escobar, visited the mansion frequently, traveling there in their private airplanes.

Griselda used the mansion as her personal house and also as the headquarters of her business. In the mansion also lived temporarily her hitmen and mules, immigrant women who worked for her. She held drugs, money, and weapons in that mansion. Some years later, the DEA confiscated the mansion and put it for sale. In 2014, the founder of Chicken Kitchen, Christian Berdouare, bought it for almost 10 million dollars. However, he only wanted to demolish it and sell the empty lot was valued at almost one million and a half more than the mansion (*La Mansión del Crimen*, 2024).

Her wealth spilled to her sons. All of them were involved in criminal activities and followed their mother's lifestyle. The three older sons, the ones she had with Trujillo, drove luxurious cars such as Lamborghini, Ferraris, and Maserati. They lived in their own mansions in Palm Island and Key Biscayne, near Griselda's, and visited their mother in their own armed jet. Young Michael Corleone lived with her mother in her mansion, and for her 6th birthday, she rented a cruise with a petting zoo for the family (Richardson, 2024).

Besides her residence in Miami, other properties also stood out for their luxury and exorbitant prices. One of them was the Coral Gables House, which was also known for the security measures around it. Griselda also had a property called the Medellin Villa. It was a one-square-mile mansion with an enormous garden in the Lombardy urbanization. Also, in the city, she bought an apartment for 25 million.

Considering the many properties, we can guess that she was very interested in real estate and concerned about how to make profitable investments. However, Griselda's interests weren't only to make clever movements to expand her wealth. She spent lots of money on out-of-control parties characterized by many excesses.

The parties in the mansion were a tragic mixture of glamour, extravagance, and violence. There would be all types of drugs, alcohol, sex, and death. Griselda would hire strippers to entertain her guests, even if she had to have them killed later. These gatherings exposed Griselda in the neighborhood and called the attention of the police. On many occasions, the neighbors called the police for the scandals and noises coming from the mansion. However, Griselda did not stop having her extreme parties. She had her own struggles with substance abuse, and she went out of control as much as the rest of the guests. However, it didn't impede her order to kill whoever she pleased.

Griselda also used the parties in her mansion to set traps for her opponents, or those she believed could be in trouble. Many of her rivals lived or ran their business near her mansions. So, she would simply ambush them and execute them in the places. On other occasions, she had to rely on more elaborate plans, yet they seemed to amuse her.

One of the most terrible attacks happened during one of those parties. Years later, one of her hitmen dubbed "El Mono" (The Monkey) recalled the aberrant facts that night. Griselda organized a party at her ranch near the village of San Cristóbal in Colombia. Some guests were inside the house, others were hanging out in the main hall gulf, while others were arriving. Suddenly, Griselda ordered El Mono to shoot four guys who were entering the property. El Mono shot them in the place in front of the astonished guests. Griselda explained they were suspects of betrayal.

After shooting at them, El Mono followed Griselda's order to remove the bodies. Then, Griselda looked at the rest of the guests and told them, "Nothing has happened here, so let us continue with the party" (Guarnizo Álvarez, 2012, para. 4).

Her parties became popular, and the media used them to portray her as the Cocaine Queen. Besides, Griselda was an inure to the most popular nightclubs, so her public profile was very noticeable. Griselda was responsible for most murders in Florida between 1979 and 1981. She killed everyone who owed her money, betrayed her, or was suspected of any act against her will. She didn't care for innocent lives that could be taken in her attacks, even if they were children (Ponti, 2024). Still, she walked freely by Miami streets, attended nightclubs, hosted the most abominable parties, and bought properties in more than one country. She might have thought she was invincible.

The Higher the Climb, the Harder the Fall

Within less than a decade, Griselda Blanco built an empire of power and wealth. She managed to live undisturbed by the authorities. Her *plata o plomo* system worked perfectly. She had the South American cartels in her hand; she succeeded in co-opting the other local stakeholders in the drug market and putting them all to her benefit; and she had driven terror to Miami streets.

Everyone with a large or little relationship with the dark world of drugs and trade centers was afraid of Griselda. An old customer, a stranger met in a bar, an acquaintance, or a potential business partner, anyone could mean entering Griselda's ring of power. And if not, any spot in a public place could unexpectedly put them on target. The only safe place was within Griselda's closest circle, but the remaining part of it was too dependent on her will and wishes.

Griselda enjoyed the life of a magnate and became one of the most prominent figures in the Florida peninsula. For years, she displayed a lifestyle of luxury and excesses. Her mansion was a no-man's land, and the only law was dictated by her whims and cruelty. The woman who came out of the deepest and most obscure holes in the Colombian suburbs, a victim of the worst crimes against a human being, had escalated to the top of the pyramid of power. She was at the peak, above everything and everyone on all sides of the law. She had created a world for herself where she had no one to fear because if she did, she just killed them. She had reached a point where she believed nothing could threaten her.

However, one way or another, power finds its limits. Every powerful person in history eventually found a wall they clashed against. There is always someone who will not buy their dignity, someone who won't put a price on their values, someone who isn't afraid of dying or doesn't actually care where the bullet is coming from. There is a moment when the most solid loyalties fall weak. People in power, like Griselda, are so engaged playing to be God, feeling so all-mighty that they forget that in the end, they are just human beings that can be seen, heard, and caught.

For years, the authorities seemed to be bound hand and foot, but sooner or later, they would find a way to reach Griselda. She was powerful, but in front of her, there was the DEA and the government of the United States. Griselda perhaps never expected that the DEA and the government would agree to play under her own rules. The cat-and-mouse game started and quickly intensified. Griselda thought she was the only one capable of corrupting the enemies. She didn't know that the cat had infiltrated her own lines and the cheese and traps were within her fortress' walls.

CHAPTER 6
THE DOWNFALL OF THE COCAINE QUEEN

Griselda looked at Miami and the whole drug market from the highs of her empire. She had everything she wanted: money, luxury, subjects, people who killed and died for her, a thorough understanding of the intricacies of law, crime, and power, and an insatiable thirst for more. Perhaps it was her ambition that pushed her beyond the limits. It isn't uncommon that the greatest leaders tend to lose contact with reality and miscalculate the risks and outcomes of their actions.

Two major factors determined Griselda's fall: her complacency and the shift in her enemies' strategy. First, Griselda got used to killing people who weren't looked for, defrauding, extorting, and stealing from others like her who couldn't reach the police. At some point, she stopped covering her traces and didn't pay enough attention to the loose ends. On the other hand, the authorities realized that filling out forms and staying attached to the standard procedures always led them to the weakest links of the chain. If they wanted to reach the big fish, they had to taint their suitcases and get into the mud.

For a long time, the DEA and the police devoted more efforts to those involved in the smuggling of cocaine and other drugs into the United States. They collaborated closely with Latin American governments, providing them with high-tech equipment and training people to fight a war on drugs in those territories. In the United States, the key was in the trading and distribution net. It took some time for the authorities to understand that the different centers were interconnected dots, and it took them even longer to realize that the mastermind behind the tangled net of violence, money, and drugs was a woman: Griselda, the Cocaine Godmother.

Eventually, the DEA found a way to unravel the thread and use Griselda's own methods to un-tie the knots to corner her. Nonetheless, Griselda proved once more to be resourceful and adaptive. She fell, and her empire crumbled, but she always had more cards to play. She managed to keep a share of power until the last minute.

The Persecution

The DEA and the governments of the United States and Colombia took over a year to finally put Griselda's empire to an end. The persecution formally started on October 4, 1974, when the DEA issued a fugitive report on Griselda. Then, she was added to the list of the National Criminal Information System and the Treasury Enforcement Communications System. The DEA had the official warrant to arrest Griselda (*United States of America, Appellee, v. Griselda Blanco*, 1988).

For years, she managed her million-dollar business, hired hitmen, and executed people at her private scandalous parties and in daylight at public places. Griselda didn't seem much concerned about keeping her head down, at least not for many years.

The DEA had a tough task in chasing Griselda; it was a game of cat and mouse. The police knew there was a mastermind behind the scenes, pulling the strings, but they weren't sure of their identity. It couldn't be a person who wasn't afraid of calling the police's attention with noisy gatherings at her mansion. It couldn't be someone who didn't cover their tracks. It couldn't be a woman. Griselda would later tell her close people that it was all part of her strategy. She knew nobody would suspect a woman. Even if they had her name on the list, they were after a different profile.

Eventually, the DEA realized that the responsible for the wave of crimes in Florida and the flood of drugs into the US market was the same person, and that was a woman: Griselda Blanco. Then, the operations to capture her intensified, and Griselda started to hide and run. She had to leave behind her life as a celebrity, as the Cocaine Queen or the Godmother and became a fugitive. She knew that she couldn't remain either in her mansion or in Miami because that made her easy prey.

As the DEA and the Florida police increased the operations and controls persecuting her, Griselda became a fugitive. Nelson Andrew, a homicide detective, explained in an interview that the two forces started working collaboratively to tighten the net around Griselda. Even if they didn't immediately catch her, they succeeded in depriving her of her personal guard and significantly limited her freedom to operate as she had enjoyed until then.

She thought that moving to the other side of the country would take the spotlight off her. Then, she settled in Irving, California, in a quiet neighborhood far away from the luxury and excesses of the old times. She settled in an apartment with a woman who presumably was her mother, though there are no details of how their relationship unfolded after Griselda ran away from her childhood home. Also, Griselda had taken with her, Michael Corleone, her younger son.

Once in California, Griselda felt safe and empowered again. She started building her business there while her elder son, Dixon Trujillo Blanco, was already settled in San Francisco. He was already running a profitable business, selling over 600 pounds of cocaine, while his brother in Miami held the business with 440 pounds a month, according to official records. Meanwhile, the other son settled a headquarters in Los Angeles and folded over 1,100 pounds of cocaine monthly (Univision Noticias, 2024). Griselda had good reasons to believe she still had the resources to reestablish her power.

However, what Griselda didn't know was that the DEA and Florida police had reached out to other states to contribute to her persecution. Eventually, it was one man's determination that eventually allowed the DEA to find and capture Griselda. Robert Palombo was an agent of the DEA who was early engaged in going after her. Somehow, Palombo became obsessed with Griselda and wouldn't stop until finding her.

The Obstacles to the Investigation

Palombo struggled to track Griselda. In the past, she had mocked the U.S. authorities and had escaped to Colombia, going unnoticed in the airport. Back then, the DEA had also listed Griselda on the wanted list. The DEA placed Blanco's name on watchlists for passports and visas to monitor her identity and appearance.

It was a real possibility that Griselda had fled to her country. It was safer for her because the Colombian government hadn't signed an extradition treaty, meaning that the DEA could not arrest Griselda in Colombian territory, or if they did, she had to be judged under Colombian laws and incarcerated in a Colombian prison. In fact, the DEA's warrant for her arrest didn't include a request for extradition.

The DEA had outdated information, and a lack of cooperation between the Colombian and the U.S. governments obstructed the procedure. When Griselda was in Colombia in the late 1970s, she told her inner circle that she wouldn't go back to the United States because she was aware that the DEA was after her. Cecil, a DEA informant, told Palombo that Griselda might have fled to Costa Rica. Palombo's job started checking the Colombian consulate trying to find out if Griselda had been issued a visa. In the end, it was all a waste of time. During that time, Griselda had settled her headquarters in her mansion in Miami, and her business was rising to its peak.

Until 1984, there was no extradition treatment between Colombia and the United States, so Palombo had good reasons to believe Griselda could be hiding in her country. Many of the DEA's efforts were misdirected in trying to trace Griselda where she wasn't. While they followed the wrong clues, Griselda amassed a fortune, threw extravagant lustful parties in her mansion, and deployed unlimited violence, executing enemies, allies, and innocent victims.

Everything changed in 1984. On May 30, Palombo had fresh data. He learned that Griselda was in Newport Beach, California. She was probably seen while visiting one of her sons. In fact, Palombo was also investigating his smuggling activity on the West side of the country. Despite he knew where she was, Palombo received the order not to arrest her. Some years later, Palombo testified in a trial and claimed that DEA authorities alleged that an attempt to arrest her at that moment would hamper the whole investigation to dismantle the network established by Griselda and her sons. Palombo had to wait to put Griselda behind bars.

Palombo had no more clues about Griselda's whereabouts, though it was certain that she wasn't in Florida and she hadn't fled to Colombia. At least she was cornered on the West Coast, but she was using a fake identity and had forged identification. In September 1984, a witness saw Griselda delivering money to a DEA informant. Griselda's power was significantly reduced, but she still had enough resources to buy wills and avoid the law. For a long time, Palombo had no way to reach Griselda's address or telephone number (*United States of America, Appellee, v. Griselda Blanco*, 1988).

DEA's Strategies

One of the hardest obstacles faced by the DEA to track criminals like Griselda was that nobody wanted to talk against them, either because they got paid for their silence or they had been involved in any of the crimes—as mules or as contract killers—or were simply too afraid of retaliation. The DEA implemented two strategies to cope with those obstacles: they used the protected witnesses program and a hotline where people could make anonymous calls to provide information or report anything related to drug dealing.

In October 1984, a woman phoned the Miami police station. She was concerned that her daughter was dating a Colombian drug trafficker. That was the first clue that would eventually lead the authorities to Griselda. The trafficker that the woman was concerned about was Uber Trujillo, Griselda's son.

Palombo used that information to trace the whole family, starting with Uber and reaching Griselda in Irving. He was appointed to monitor her exclusively, but despite many attempts, he struggled to approach enough. On one occasion, Griselda arranged an appointment with a DEA agent at the Marriott hotel in Newport Beach. They met in the lobby, and Griselda offered him a significant amount of money. She wanted him to get her an official ID and become legal again.

Palombo was close to arresting her that time, but the operation failed. The agent didn't want to risk the whole operation and reveal the identity of a secret informant who was cooperating with them. So, Griselda escaped once more, but her money was no longer enough to get her whatever she wanted.

A few months later, Palombo had already identified the house where Griselda was living and launched a full operation to arrest her there. On February 17, 1985, a DEA squad arrived at the house and knocked on Griselda's door. She was home.

The Arrest

The agents entered the house, and Palombo found her in her bedroom. She was reading the Bible. Palombo confronted her and said: "Hello, Griselda. We finally meet" (Sáez, 2024, para. 3). She calmly answered also in Spanish: "No, my name is Betty" (Sáez, 2024, para. 3). But Palombo was quite certain that he had the right woman. Other sources indicate she said she was named Patty and was a Venezuelan housewife (Univision Noticias, 2024).

The DEA agents inspected the house and found Griselda's belongings. She had a forged passport and a .38-caliber pistol that proved she was who Palombo claimed she was. Years later, Colombo recalled the moment of the arrest. He said Griselda didn't abandon her defiant look and attitude but it completely changed when she was introduced in the patrol car. He sat with her in the back seat and observed her. He noticed that then, Griselda realized that it was all over. Her life as the Cocaine Queen had ended.

Palombo said about Griselda at that moment when they were taking her, finally under arrest (Bell & Veloso, 2024):

We drove up to Los Angeles, and when we got close to the courthouse, she became visibly shaken, [...] I mean, visibly shaken, she was shaking, and she grabbed my arm, and you could feel her shaking, and she turned, and she threw up on my shoulder. Not a lot, it was mostly just bile, but she knew the proverbial s*** had hit the fan (para. 5).

However, Griselda would soon confirm that her luck hadn't completely abandoned her. Palombo would realize that despite all his efforts, Griselda would somehow get away with it. For all the crimes she had. They, she would be given capital punishment or, at least, a life sentence. For the crimes the justice could prove, she would get a much more benevolent sentence.

The Trial

Griselda had committed enough crimes to be indicted for several sentences. However, for the judicial system, it isn't enough that the crimes have been committed; justice must prove them. The first indictment against Griselda Blanco was in 1975, but she fled to Colombia then.

She was charged with "conspiring to manufacture, import into the United States, and distribute cocaine. By January 1976, twelve of the conspirators had been prosecuted and convicted, and two others had pleaded guilty" (United States v Blanco, 2006, para. 1). However, by that time, there was no treaty of extradition between the Colombian government and the United States, so the possibilities for the DEA to trace her in her homeland were limited.

The DEA had to wait until Griselda went back to the United States to capture her, finally. When they finally did, Agent Palombo had to gather all the evidence so she would receive a fair sentence.

The Prosecution's Strategy and Griselda's Effective Defense

The trial began on June 25, 1985, and it was held before Judge Cannella. For two weeks, the prosecutor tried to prove Griselda was guilty of an extensive list of crimes and tried to support the evidence with significant testimonials. The prosecution focused on the testimonial of a woman who knew Griselda from her early days. Her name was Carmen Caban, a former drug dealer who accepted to testify against Griselda in exchange for a lower sentence for herself. This was one of the government's strategies to gather witnesses that could prove Griselda's guilt.

The government had already gathered evidence against Caban, and that was used to press her to collaborate. Eventually, Caban told the jury the details of Griselda's operations between 1972 and 1975, when she was barely building her empire. Caban confessed to having been part of Griselda's drug smuggling network. However, Griselda's defense managed to use this as an argument to override Caban's testimonials. Griselda's lawyers proved that Caban had obtained not only immunity for her crimes. The lawyers presented evidence to prove that the government had paid a large amount of money to Caban to ensure she would testify against Griselda.

Moreover, the defense claimed that Caban was a drug dealer with an extensive list of crimes. Since she had been involved in the smuggling network, she had personal interests in Griselda's condemnation. Thus, Caban's testimonial could be considered as part of her own defensive strategy. Even though this didn't prove Griselda's innocence, it was a powerful argument to weaken evidence against her: "Judge Cannella prevented defense counsel from asking Caban about her alleged participation in a murder, ruling that the prejudice caused by testimony about this matter would far outweigh its probative value" (United States of America, Appellee, v. Griselda Blanco, 1988, para. 9).

This dismantled this part of the prosecutor's strategy against Griselda because the judge's denial also banned another key witness, Carmen Caban's sister. Gloria Caban was another witness who would testify about Griselda's early crimes, but Judge Canella dismissed her. Despite the endless list of crimes, the prosecution had little evidence to achieve the desired sentence.

As the trial progressed, the prosecution's arguments fell one by one. Eventually, the judge admitted evidence that proved Griselda was carrying false identification at the moment of her arrest. The prosecution aimed to prove that Griselda was deliberately covering her identity because she was hiding from the law. Thus, it should be considered evidence that proved she was aware of her crimes and assumed to be guilty.

It wasn't enough. Judge Canella considered that using a fake identity wasn't strong enough evidence to prove somebody's guilt. Moreover, he elaborated on diverse reasons why an innocent person would attempt to cover their true identity. The judge instructed the jury to carefully examine if that piece of evidence consistently indicated a consciousness of guilt (*United States of America, Appellee, v. Griselda Blanco*, 1988). The prosecution lacked a strong plea to persuade them that Griselda was indeed covering her identity because she was broadly aware of the consequences she faced.

Other Witnesses and Further Evidence

The prosecution worked to sustain Caban's testimonial. They aimed to prove her participation in Griselda's drug trading network. They brought to the stand people who had collaborated with Griselda as couriers and seizures of drugs. They had also gathered evidence of conversations between the Cocaine Godmother and other dealers. These pieces of evidence were all related to Griselda's crimes between 1972 and 1975. This means that they had nothing against her for the most terrible crimes she had committed when established in Miami.

However, all the efforts were put to find something that could lead to a sentence that meant prison. Thus, the prosecution presented as evidence the arrest of Antonio Romero in 1972. According to the prosecution, Romero's case proved the charges of conspiracy against Griselda. He had been arrested at Kennedy Airport with a dog cage. Inside it, he carried a significant amount of cocaine he was trying to smuggle into the United States. He was alleged to be a member of Griselda's criminal ring. Romero was supposed to be the proof of Griselda's connection with the Colombian cartel.

Nonetheless, Judge Canella once more alleged that it wasn't enough since they had to demonstrate four elements: agreement, overt acts, violation of the law, and the accused person's participation. Canella told the jury during the trial (*United States of America, Appellee, v. Griselda Blanco*, 1988):

the government must prove here there is one conspiracy, namely, that the drugs were gotten in Columbia [sic], brought in through Miami or other places, and then brought to New York. That is the conspiracy that is charged, and that is the conspiracy they must prove, a single conspiracy... (para. 12).

Once more, the prosecution's strategy was torn to pieces, and still, they had nothing to obtain an exemplary sentence. At some point, it seemed Griselda was about to walk out of the courtroom as a free woman. All the crimes she had committed meant nothing if they couldn't be proved at trial.

Besides dismantling all the witnesses the prosecution brought to the stand, Griselda's defense also had a more offensive strategy. They didn't only focus on rejecting evidence that pointed to Griselda's guilt; they tried to prove that the government had treated her unfairly. The defense aimed to label the case as invalid because Griselda had been denied essential rights.

The defense stated that the government had violated her right to a speedy trial as it is warranted in the Sixth Amendment and under the former rules of the circuit where the trial was held. According to the defense, the trial and the full indictment should be dismissed. This would have broad implications not only because she would walk free but also because she couldn't be judged in the future for those crimes.

Griselda's defense claimed that the DEA had deliberately postponed her arrest and, consequently, her trial. They had not arrested her when she was in Colombia, even though the reason behind that was the lack of an extradition agreement. Moreover, Griselda claimed that they refused to arrest her in Newport Beach in May 1984, even though they had identified her. Instead, they delayed the operation for nine months. Her defense aimed to make this appear as a factor that a speed trial would have benefitted her.

The DEA had to provide substantial explanations of the reasons behind that decision to refute Griselda's defense's argument. Then, the argument was that a premature arrest would ruin the whole operation that was deployed to uncover her smuggling network and her sons' also engaged in the business. Moreover, a shift in the plan hampered the informant's life. Eventually, this confirmed Griselda's defense's argument: the DEA had her and chose not to arrest her.

Nonetheless, considering previous cases and the validity of the government's arguments, the delay in the trial didn't violate any duty of diligence (*United States of America, Appellee, v. Griselda Blanco*, 1988).

Moreover, the prosecution was able to turn this argument against Griselda. During the nine months between the DEA's first discovery of her presence in California and the moment of her arrest, Griselda lived under a fake identity. That revealed her will to avoid the law. She had deliberately chosen to be a fugitive and, therefore, never showed the will to submit herself to the United States government and accept a trial, speed or not.

Despite this one was a solid argument, the defense still had another card to play. They alleged that she had not behaved as a fugitive. They relied on a previous case, United States v. Salzmann, 548 F.2d 395, 403 n. 2 (2d Cir. 1976). In this case, a Judge's footnote stated that the accused had not acted as a fugitive since he had not hidden or rejected being taken to trial. Griselda's defense, then, stated that she had never meant to remain hidden from the authorities as she lived her life as any other citizen (*United States of America, Appellee, v. Griselda Blanco*, 1988). There were many possible reasons why she used another name or didn't reveal where she lived, as Judge Canella had explained to the trial jury. As they concealed, the U.S. government knew where she lived in Colombia, and still, there was no arrest. They knew where to find her in Newport Beach, and again, they didn't go for her. It wasn't Griselda who had avoided being taken on trial; the DEA had delayed her trial. No accused is forced to act against their benefit.

However, the evidence against Griselda was enough to prove that she had actually acted as a fugitive. When she left the United States to flee to Colombia in the 1970s, she did it under a fake identity with a forged passport and had never explicitly expressed her will to appear for trial. Thus, neither the trial nor the indictment was dismissed, and the jury arrived at a sentence, though it was far from what was expected.

The Sentence

Before the trial, Griselda Blanco was expected to receive the worst of punishments. She was responsible for even more crimes. It is believed to have been directly implicated in over 200 crimes, not considering the many lives that were also impacted by her drug business. According to Drugs in American Society, "she was responsible for most of South Florida's murders from 1979 to 1981. She was also behind the 1982 death of a 2-year-old who was an accidental casualty in her attempted takedown of a rival" (Biography.com Editors & Kettler, 2024, para. 8). The boy was one of Griselda's former hitman and was shot in his head while traveling in his father's car.

Nonetheless, she was sentenced on one count of conspiracy to manufacture, import into the United States, and cocaine distribution. In the end, the court denied Griselda's claim to dismiss the trial and sentenced her to 15 years in prison and a $25,000 fine (*United States v Blanco*, 2006), nothing compared to the fortune she gathered during her years as the Cocaine Queen.

Meanwhile, her defense would continue their attempt to take Griselda out of prison. In fact, the Cocaine Queen was wounded by not dead: She still had power and resources she wouldn't hesitate to use to achieve her freedom. There is no firm evidence, but several sources reported that while in prison, she ordered her people to kidnap John F. Kennedy Jr. Her plan was to bribe the authorities: She would trade the former president's son for her freedom (Biography.com Editors & Kettler, 2024).

Eventually, the plan didn't work out, and Griselda would spend a long time in prison, even more than what was stated in the first sentence. However, she never stopped running her business even being incarcerated (Tikkanen, n.d.).

Life in Prison

The legal procedures didn't end with the sentence. The authorities continued with the investigation to prove Griselda's responsibility for some of the many murders. She was later indicted of three counts of first-degree murder. West Miami Police Chief Nelson Andreu had not dropped his commitment to make Griselda pay for all the crimes she committed in Florida.

Once more, the authorities sought to present evidence against Griselda from the people who knew her the most and had witnessed her crimes firsthand. Nonetheless, also Griselda's defense found once more a way to revert them.

A Key Betrayal

Andreu thought it wasn't enough to have Griselda in prison; there was a case for cocaine smuggling and murder that remained buried in the Orlando State Attorney's office. Seven boxes with evidence and reports of the most terrible crimes were stored while Griselda paid a sentence for minor crimes instead of facing the electric chair. Andreu insisted and revitalized the case to request Griselda be judged and sentenced for the rest of the crimes. The CBS4 invested several days compiling evidence linking Blanco to over a dozen homicides. Ultimately, prosecutors pursued charges against her for only three of those cases (*Griselda Blanco: Escaping The Electric Chair*, 2012).

One of those cases was particularly relevant because it directly implicated one of Griselda's closest men. The case was the murder of Johnny Castro. He was a two-year-old boy, son of one of Griselda's hitmen, Jesus Castro. The man had committed the unforgettable mistake of refusing to follow her orders. Griselda wanted him to collaborate with one of her sons. At Castro's denial, Griselda sent Rivi Ayala to execute him.

However, things didn't go the expected way. Ayala rode a motorbike, reached Castro's car, and shot. Castro was taking his little son to McDonalds. The bullet that was supposed to punish the rebel hitmen reached the wrong victim, and the child was dead.

Ayala said later, when he was caught, that Griselda was very upset to find out they had failed their mission. They learned they had killed the wrong person when the case reached the news. However, neither of them thought about the consequences it would have.

Castro left the body of his son wrapped in a blanket and his documents at a mosque in Miami. He wanted the police to find him and eventually, it would take them to Ayala and Griselda. The case remained unsolved for many years, but then Castro was caught by the police, and his testimonials took the police directly to Ayala. It was a chance to prove a charge of murder against Griselda.

The other case against Griselda was for the murder of a couple, Alfredo and Gisel Lorenzo. They were killed while their three children watched television in the living room. Ayala was also appointed to this mission, as Andreu explained later (*Griselda Blanco: Escaping The Electric Chair*, 2012):

Alfredo Lorenzo owed Griselda some money for some drugs she had given him. The drugs were either stolen, or the money was stolen. He couldn't pay for them. The instructions to Ayala were, "Go there, get my money. If you can't get my money, then you kill him. And you kill everybody."

After many years, the evidence gathered from those cases took the police to Jorge Rivi Ayala. The police decided to use Ayala as an instrument to finally condemn Griselda for the many terrible crimes she committed. They offered him a reduction in his own sentence if he agreed to collaborate.

Ayala had been Griselda's main hitman and man of trust for many years. He had been in charge of her most important missions and knew her criminal network to the detail. His testimonial would be definitely persuasive to the jury, and Griselda would inevitably be sentenced to death.

Griselda was paying her sentence in a federal prison. The new evidence and a new case filed against her took her back to Miami, and she had to appear in court once more. She was charged with three murders—Johnny Castro and the Lorenzo couple—and there was a significant possibility of facing a death sentence. The prosecution's stellar witness was Griselda's star hitman, Rivi Ayala.

Andreu explained that Ayala's testimonial was almost the only evidence against Griselda, so anything that could hamper his credibility could take the case back to cero. Andreu said, "There was no DNA. There were no fingerprints. There was very little physical ballistics. I don't know if we had any evidence we could even match at the time... So the case rested on Jorge Ayala's credibility and reliability" (*Griselda Blanco: Escaping The Electric Chair, 2012*, para. 44).

Nonetheless, Griselda's defense found a way to undermine Ayala's testimonial. They discovered Ayala had sex phone with the attorney's secretary, Sherry Rossback. The woman said that it was part of the prosecution attorney's strategies to persuade Ayala to convey more sensitive information to incriminate Griselda. The prosecutor didn't confirm her declarations (Tikkanen, n.d.), and Ayala's credibility fainted.

This turn of events tore down the prosecutor's strategy. Again, they had barely anything. Eventually, they offered Griselda's defense a deal. She accepted the charges and received a minor sentence, and they stopped filing cases against her. Griselda accepted the deal, and in 1998, the jury found her guilty of three second-degree murders.

Nonetheless, Griselda wouldn't complete her sentence in jail.

Griselda's Fourth Partner

Even in prison, Griselda didn't stop being any of the things she had been outside. She didn't give up her business, and she continued having romantic affairs as in the old ties of the Black Widow. While in jail, she met Charles Cosby, her fourth partner. Unlike the others, she didn't marry him and failed to assassinate him.

Charles Cosby was a lowly drug dealer. He was only 20 years old when he met Griselda. He knew about her from what he heard in the news and became fascinated by her figure and story. She had everything he wanted. He was so captivated by Griselda that he wrote her a letter in prison.

Griselda answered back and started a romantic relationship, only exchanging letters. In 1991, Cosby went to prison and visited Griselda. Then, they took the relationship to the next stage. Cosby said in an interview that Griselda paid significant amounts of money to the guards to allow them to have intimate encounters in a closet.

According to Cosby's story, they had over 300 encounters in prison. He was in love with her, probably dominated by Griselda's overwhelming figure and power. He said that they wanted to get married and that Griselda always spoke about their future together (Jiménez, 2024).

However, Cosby's interest in Griselda was probably fueled by her fortune. Cosby admitted that Griselda bought him $20,000 Rolex, and also a $55,000 Mercedes. Over time, Griselda made Cosby a millionaire (Jiménez, 2024).

The relationship lasted about a year. It came to an end when Griselda hired a hitman to kill Cosby. She had found out he had a parallel relationship with a blonde woman. Cosby was driving his car when a motorbike stopped by him at the traffic lights. The hitmen shoot him four times. Nonetheless, Cosby was luckier than

Griselda's first three husbands. He was wearing a bulletproof vest that absorbed the bullets and saved his life.

Sometime later, Cosby visited Griselda in prison. She was furious because she was aware of his affair with the other woman and because her people failed to kill him. So, she tried to do the thing on her own. As Cosby entered the room, she went over to him and tried to strangle him. The guard intervened and took Griselda off him. That was the last time Cosby and Griselda were together. It was just good luck that saved him from becoming the Black Widow's fourth victim.

Griselda's Sons' Fate

While Griselda was in prison, everything else kept on working. Her business was still running and her sons were in charge of the new connections. Griselda still had power, but it wasn't enough to protect them. The three sons she had with Trujillo were killed while she was in prison, and there was nothing she could do to avoid it.

Hypothesis about what happened to Griselda's sons are varied. It is known that Dixon and Osvaldo were also captured by the DEA. All of them, Griselda and her sons, were sent to prison almost at the same time. Nonetheless, Dixon and Osvaldo used their right to parole and were set free in 1992. That same year, Osvaldo was assassinated in a nightclub in Colombia. Later, it is alleged that Griselda's son, Uber, was also executed. Much later, after Griselda was released, Dixon was also shot while he was walking in the street (Ellis, 2024). The only son who survived Griselda was the youngest, Michael Corleone Blanco.

Back to the Starting Line

The empire was turned to ashes. The Miami cartel plummeted. Griselda Blanco was no longer the most powerful drug boss in the business. After a rocketing career with mind-blowing outcomes in terms of money and bloodshed in the streets, Griselda Blanco ended up behind bars. Did the good guys triumph over evil? Did the victims finally find peace and justice? That is not so clear.

Griselda had to put down her life as a celebrity; certainly, the power of using a personal army to get rid of whoever she pointed out and move large amounts of money belonged to the past. However, many versions insisted on pointing out that her days as the Cocaine Godmother hadn't ended after all. She was only judged for a bunch of crimes that were just the tip of the iceberg. The judicial system didn't have the means to dive deeper into her endless criminal record. It was enough to keep her in jail for over 20 years but, did she truly pay for her crimes? Did she ever stop being the cruel and ruthless boss of the drug trading network?

Several sources alleged that she continued to be the head of the criminal organization even while in jail. She still had her connections within and outside the prison, and unfortunately, the "*plata o plomo*" formula worked also along the prison corridors and cells. Griselda still held the reins of part of the business and still had the ability to allocate her money, either to pay for more killings or to keep it safe from the authorities.

Despite all this, Griselda in prison was just a shadow of the Cocaine Godmother of the old times. Even though most of her crimes were never uncovered and she received no punishment for them, her health deteriorated, and she eventually obtained freedom again, only to see how she was dragged back to the same place where everything began. It was a resounding defeat.

In the end, Griselda managed to mock justice. She didn't even pay for her sentence completely. But freedom only caused her to come back to the same streets where she started as a pickpocket and a prostitute. All she had gone through, all the blood and death she spread, served for nothing. Aged and ill, Griselda found herself roaming the same neighborhoods until she found death in her own rules.

CHAPTER 7
THE END

Throughout her life, Griselda had showcased many well-defined qualities. She was intelligent, reckless, strong, and, most of all, persistent. Despite all the challenges and threats she confronted, she never gave up on her objectives, deadly and ambitious objectives. She didn't stop until dominating the streets of the capital of the drug market, forced all the major cartels that were at war against each other to obey her, and made the market march at the pace she marked.

Being captured by the DEA was a tough strike for her, but on that occasion, she didn't give up either. She fought back to be released from the first moment. Many can be surprised that she didn't show remorse or guilt for everything she had done. It is hard to say. Every person would fight for their freedom under any circumstance. However, Griselda always seemed to be persuaded that nothing she had done could compensate for all the world owed to her due to the horrible life she had been trapped in since she could remember.

From the moment of her arrest until the day she was conceded freedom, she struggled to be set free. And for that, she relied on what she had turned her back a very long time ago: law and justice.

She and her defense tried to use every available resource and legal gap that could help her walk out of prison. Meanwhile, the DEA and justice sought a way to harden the sentences, even gathering testimonials from her own personal army and old loyal hitman Ravi Ayala. At that point, Griselda's unconventional resources didn't work. It was Griselda's own body, her weak and human part, that eventually served as an escape gate back to freedom.

However, Griselda carried her past and her crimes wherever she went. The shadows of all she had done hadn't disappeared and were waiting for her. If justice had failed to punish her enough, destiny and the law of the street would secure she paid all her debts.

The Release

When the DEA and Agent Palombo chased Griselda and finally arrested her, they expected the maximum sentence. Instead of capital punishment or, at least, a life sentence, she was only going to spend 15 years. Most of her crimes, the cruelest, couldn't be proven, and that's justice. The punishment is based not on what the accused did, but on what the prosecution can effectively prove. Any detail or slight evidence that can benefit the accused is used to smooth the sentence. Eventually, Griselda walked almost unpunished for the dozens of murders, extortion, and torture of all of her victims.

The few years added for the three-murder trial served more to show she wasn't over as a powerful criminal leader. Instead of showcasing that justice never stops hunting the criminals, the trial served to expose the flaws in the judicial system, and Griselda had an opportunity that even in jail, she still had resources to negotiate with the government. In the end, the sentence was set under her rules.

Griselda left behind her throne as the Cocaine Queen in Florida, but kept most of her real power within a federal prison. She was out of the streets, but that didn't mean the weakening of her drug trading net. On the contrary, it served to prove that the system was so solidly established that she could simply manage it remotely and from within a federal prison. The system revealed itself to be weak and corruptible, a negative message for society and the other prominent drug landlords operating in the United States. Griselda could even buy presents for her boyfriend and date him whenever she wanted to be in prison.

Despite the many privileges Griselda managed to secure for herself, she never gave up her desire to be free. She never showed remorse for all the death and pain she caused. She never believed that she had a debt to pay to society. Instead, she always had a team of defense lawyers working to take her out of prison.

Griselda appealed her sentence on many occasions and insisted on the argument that the US government denied her a speed trial. She claimed that her rights had been violated, and thus, her sentence was unfair and the trial invalid. Her last attempt was to plead guilty in 1998. She tried to exchange a confession for a reduction in her sentence (Tikkanen, n.d.).

The U.S. justice never deferred to her claim. Nonetheless, Griselda eventually achieved being released before completing her sentence. In 2004, she suffered a heart attack in prison and was concealed the privilege of being released due to her health issues. Griselda was a free woman, but wouldn't enjoy full rights. The government of the United States deported her to Colombia.

Back in Medellin

There is no way to know if Griselda preferred to live in Florida or any place in the United States or go back to the country she left to escape from poverty. She had to find a place where she could be safe. She had paid her debt to the US justice, but that wasn't her main concern. She wouldn't have to be a fugitive to evade the law, but instead, she had to hide from the many enemies she reaped throughout her life, even during her years in prison.

In 2004, Griselda reallocated in Colombia, in Medellin. She went back to the same point where everything began. She didn't settle in a mansion and seemed to have left behind her opulent life. There was no trace of the powerful woman who threw parties and executed anyone who dared to defy her. She had no luxurious car and was isolated. Her sons were dead, and the youngest was trying to build a life away from his mother's reputation.

The US and the Colombian authorities could never prove if they confiscated all of Griselda's fortune. Her properties were expropriated, and she certainly didn't have any bank accounts. However, her business was active for 20 years while she was a federal inmate. Where did all that money go? Nobody knows.

It is also unknown how Griselda survived in Medellin. Some sources affirm that she lived on rent, which would mean she had kept some of her properties. There are no official records of any legal business run by Griselda. Even though she didn't openly use the money she still had, some testimonials reveal that she still had access to part of her fortune. The last thing she did was to order 300,000 pesos of meat (Guarnizo Alvarez, 2012).

Some testimonials suggest that Griselda chose to live in anonymity, but she was never poor. It was all a facade. A policeman who knew about her whereabouts in her last days told the press (Guarnizo Alvarez, 2012):

"Poor? Listen to this: you and I are poor," said a police officer. "She went around driving her Mazdita [a black Mazda 6] and collecting the money from the leases on the properties she still owned. She was also selling a building for 1,500 million pesos" (para. 15).

In her 60s, Griselda tried to live as a common woman who had little in common with the Cocaine Godmother, the reckless Queen, or the Black Widow. She had many reasons to keep a low profile. She lived in a humble neighborhood, almost in poverty, and retired from criminal life.

People who lived in her neighborhood or saw her every time to time didn't know who she truly was. Witnesses said that she was a grown-up lady who seemed to be friendly. Nobody could guess she was responsible for the massacres and atrocities in Medellin, New York, and Miami. Moreover, people around her said that she even gave money to collaborate with her community. Perhaps it was her way to seek forgiveness, perhaps she was still trying to buy others' goodwill and find peace. It didn't happen. Her fate was waiting for her.

The Last day

On September 3, 2012, Griselda Blanco left her house in Medellin and traveled to the other side of the city with an intriguing task. She went to a meatpacking house in Bethlehem district in the southwest. She reached there to take an order she had made: 300,000 pesos (140 dollars) of meat, all to be picked on the same day. What she was going to do with that amount of meat remains a mystery. There is no record of testimonials from the people at the store.

What is known is what happened next. She was sitting inside the store, waiting for the shopkeeper to deliver her order. Outside, a motorbike was parked in front of the store. At 3 PM, a young man entered and looked around. He was looking for something or someone. Everything happened within a few seconds. He was wearing a motorcycle helmet. Another one waited outside on the motorbike with the engine on.

Griselda remained still in her seat. We might wonder if she had a clue that the end was near. The image of a motorcycle rider who wouldn't take off his helmet must have reminded her of the uncountable times her men had used that suit to fulfill her deadly orders. It was her turn now.

The motorcycle rider turned his head and saw Griselda. He was looking for her. The man walked toward her, pulled out a revolver, and without saying a word, he shot her twice in the head. She didn't say anything either. Her body just felt from the chair with no sound. Griselda Blanco was 69 years old, and after a lifetime of crime, she fell victim to the same murder style she claimed to have invented. The twists of life, one might think.

The man left the place while everyone in the store was in shock. He left in the motorcycle, leaving no clues of who had ordered the murder. Shortly after, the police arrived, and they identified Griselda Blanco. She barely looked like the rude and reckless Cocaine Queen. A few minutes later, the ambulance arrived, too, and she was taken to the hospital. It was too late for her. A half-hour later, Griselda died at a nearby hospital, neither a multimillionaire still in her pomp, nor penniless as in her youth" (Guarnizo Alvarez, 2012, para. 16-17).

Who Killed Griselda?

To many, Griselda's death was a relief. Even though she had left her life as a criminal behind, she wasn't completely inactive. A lot of people still owed her money, some of them had betrayed her, and many others who had been fierce competitors wanted her out of the business. Justice had stopped looking for her, but she would never get rid of all the people she had damaged and wanted to take revenge on her.

The case of Griselda's murder wasn't followed by an exhaustive investigation. The identity of the two motormen was never discovered. It is assumed that it was, indeed, one of Griselda's enemies.

Later the day of the murder, her son Michael was at his home teaching their sons to swim. The telephone rang, and when he picked it up, a voice he didn't recognize told him: "Michael, I'm standing over your mother's dead body" (Robinson, 2024, para. 22). Michael was certain that it must have been a reckoning.

Reflecting on Griselda's murder, a specialist in organized crime wrote: "She might have retired to Colombia and wasn't anything like the kind of player she was in her early days, but she had lingering enemies almost everywhere you look. What goes around comes around" (Robinson, 2024, para. 15).

Her body was buried in the Jardines de Montesacro cemetery. It is a simple grave on the ground covered with fresh grass and a bunch of flowers on top. No signs of her power, her wealth, or her rage.

The End

If law and justice fell short of putting a sentence that compensated all the death and destruction Griselda was responsible for, life's whims took her back to the past she had tried to leave behind. Griselda died in poverty, caught by surprise, and with no chance to defend herself. She wasn't killed by the police, and none of the big fish of the drug market she had controlled.

Her killers were two hitmen on a motorbike, her cruel invention. Two people who probably took the criminal mission for a few bundles of money. Two people who probably didn't even know who she was and how she had earned such an end. Griselda's greatness had disappeared, and she wasn't even worth knowing who wanted to kill her. It could be just an ordinary robbery. Griselda Blanco wasn't the subject of interest any longer.

CONCLUSION

The tragic yet not surprising end of this tumultuous saga serves as a stark reminder of the fine line that separates power and vulnerability in the dangerous underbelly of society. Griselda Blanco's journey started on the borders of marginality in Medellin. She took in all the violence and danger around her and made it her inner strength.

Instead of fighting against such a tragic destiny, she chose to master it. She didn't run away from the shadows; instead, she did all she had to become the queen. And she succeeded. She reached the peak of power. Eventually, she received a punishment.

The lives of people like Griselda Blanco provoke opposing opinions. Some people see a monster who deserves the worst punishment. Others believed she was a byproduct of a childhood of violence and deprivation who struggled to stay alive. While she couldn't be considered innocent, it was impossible to judge her. A person who is not treated as a person will probably not feel empathy or develop sensitivity, yet it wouldn't expiate her blame.

This story has aimed to depict Griselda Blanco's life as it was, remaining faithful to facts and sources. It has not delved into moral judgment or social analysis to ponder if she was a victim of her context or the embodiment of evil. The book has covered all the relevant aspects that framed Griselda's life and contributed to shaping the decisions she made at each stage. We have unraveled the ball of threads and connections that linked her to the core of the most dangerous criminal organizations. It is difficult to distinguish if she cooperated to bring the Colombian and Mexican cartels into power or if she just got trapped after managing complex relationships with men who would have used and killed her if she hadn't done it first.

With all the information shared throughout these pages, the reader has the elements to decide which image of Griselda they will keep. Many questions will remain open: Was Griselda a monster? Did Griselda Blanco truly have other options, and did she choose a deliberate crime? Was her death nothing more than what she deserved? Was the punishment she received enough to compensate for the thousands of lives she destroyed?

The life of Griselda Blanco confronts us with a woman who defied society's norms, with no scrupulous or limits; she was only moved by her own ambitions and desires. She died under her own rules, but we still might wonder if it was a fair price for her to pay.

Controversial lives such as Blanco's story invite deeper reflections about our perceptions of morality, power, and the lengths people will go to carve their own path, particularly those who come from the corners of society after years of suffering aggression and suppression.

Griselda Blanco stands out for being a woman, a pioneer, and the most powerful drug boss in the 1970s and 1980s. However, she wasn't the only one: She was surrounded by subjects, allies, and enemies who worked with her to shape a world in which drug dealing became just another profitable business. Other names of the other cartel leaders are relevant pieces to understand this puzzle that is organized crime.

This book doesn't pursue the social objective of raising awareness of the dangers of extreme poverty as the breeding ground for drug consumption and escalation of violence. Griselda Blanco is just one interesting story that deserves to be told for itself. However, we are inevitably encouraged to reflect on these types of controversial characters that depict a dark side of human nature and social dynamics. Griselda Blanco's life and death showcase the intricate paths to power and wealth that we might believe are just possible in fiction but are even crueler in real life. On different levels and with limited or broader consequences, people are constantly confronted with difficult choices framed by fate or reason, all of us are driven by the human impulse to survive and get some control in a chaotic world.

REFERENCES

Barry Seal. (n.d.). *Spartacus Educational.* https://spartacus-educational.com/JFKseal.htm

Bell, C. & Veloso, L. (2024, January 29). *How was Griselda Blanco caught? She evaded authorities for 10 years.* Style Caster. https://stylecaster.com/entertainment/tv-movies/1703427/how-griselda-blanco-caught/

Berti, A. (2020, April 6). *Timeline: the history of airport body scanners.* Airport Technology. https://www.airport-technology.com/features/history-of-body-scanners/

Biography.com Editors & Kettler, S. (2024, January 25). *Griselda Blanco.* Biography. https://www.biography.com/crime/griselda-blanco

Bravo, E. (2021, September 10). *Los últimos Cocaine Cowboys: Así fue la vida loca de Sal Magluta y Willy Falcón.* GQ. https://www.revistagq.com/noticias/articulo/cocaine-cowboys-miami-netflix

Britto, L. (2020, November). *Marijuana Boom: The rise and fall of Colombia's first drug paradise.* CLC Books. https://clcjbooks.rutgers.edu/books/marijuana-boom-the-rise-and-fall-of-colombias-first-drug-paradise/

Catiang, P. (2018, November 18). *King of sea and sky: tracing Escobar's drug routes by the vehicles and tactics he used.* ABS-CBN. https://www.abs-cbn.com/ancx/culture/spotlight/11/18/18/the-king-of-sea-and-sky

Clawson, P.L. & Lee, R.W. (1996). The Medellín and Cali Cartels. In: The Andean cocaine industry. *Palgrave Macmillan, New York.* https://doi.org/10.1007/978-1-349-60978-9_2

The Cocaine Godmother. (n.d.). Crime Museum. https://www.crimemuseum.org/crime-library/drugs/the-cocaine-godmother/#google_vignette

The Colombian Cartels. (n.d.). PBS. https://create.dibbly.com/d/SLWARNxojO5iTgjWdq5J

Córdoba, A. & Roche, C. (2024, February 26). *Did Griselda Blanco and Pablo Escobar meet in real life? What was their relationship?* AS. https://en.as.com/entertainment/did-griselda-blanco-and-pablo-escobar-meet-in-real-life-what-was-their-relationship-n/

Diaz Pascual, I. (2021, June 29). America's War on Drugs — 50 years later. *The Leadership Conference on Civil and Human Rights.* https://civilrights.org/blog/americas-war-on-drugs-50-years-later/

Djangi, P. (2024, February 5). *Ascenso y caída de Griselda Blanco, la "madrina" de la cocaína de los 70.* National Geographic. https://www.nationalgeographic.es/historia/2024/02/griselda-blanco-quien-fue-madrina-cocaina-70

Drake, L.R. & Scott, P.J.H. (2018, April, 24). DARK classics in chemical neuroscience: Cocaine. *ACS Chem Neurosci, 9*(10):2358-2372. doi: 10.1021/acschemneuro.8b00117

Drug Enforcement Administration. (n.d.). History. https://www.dea.gov/sites/default/files/2021-04/1975-1980_p_39-49.pdf

Drug mule Bell and Bridle. (n.d.). DEA Museum. https://museum.dea.gov/museum-collection/collection-spotlight/artifact/drug-mule-bell-bridle

The Editors of the Encyclopedia Britannica. (n.d.). War on Drugs. In *Encyclopedia Britannica.* February 20, 2025. https://www.britannica.com/topic/war-on-drugs

Elguera, S. (2023, August 11). *Rivi Ayala: The tragic journey of a Cocaine Cowboys hitman.* Medium. https://medium.com/@saloskys/rivi-ayala-the-tragic-journey-of-a-cocaine-cowboys-hitman-8b938bdeaf95

Elguera, S. (2023, August 11). The rise and fall of Mickey Munday: A Cocaine Cowboy's tale. Medium. https://medium.com/@saloskys/title-the-rise-and-fall-of-mickey-munday-a-cocaine-cowboys-tale-d25e9bc69fc4

Ellis, P. (2024, December 3). *Here's what happened to each of Griselda Blanco's sons.* Men's Health. https://www.menshealth.com/uk/entertainment/a63084729/griselda-blanco-sons/

Ellis, P. (2024, February 1). *Did crime boss Griselda Blanco really have her husband killed?* Men's Health. https://www.menshealth.com/entertainment/a46583307/griselda-blanco-husbands-dario-sepulveda/

Freixes, J. (2024, May 11). *Griselda Blanco: Pablo Escobar's narco 'Godmother.'* Colombia. https://colombiaone.com/2024/05/11/griselda-blanco/

González, P. (2021, August 5). *Cocaine Cowboys: qué pasó con los criminales del mayor caso de drogas de Miami.* GQ. https://www.gq.com.mx/entretenimiento/articulo/cocaine-cowboys-quienes-son-donde-estan-ahora-documental-netflix#:~:text=En%20los%20a%C3%B1os%2080%2C

Griselda Blanco. (n.d.). Find a Grave. https://es.findagrave.com/memorial/96527921/griselda-blanco/photo

Griselda Blanco: Escaping the electric chair. (2012, November 20). CBS News. https://www.cbsnews.com/miami/news/griselda-blanco-escaping-the-electric-chair/

Guarnizo Álvarez, J. (2012, September 13). *Colombia's "cocaine queen" living in obscurity when she was shot dead.* El País. https://english.elpais.com/elpais/2012/09/13/inenglish/1347536945_696771.html

Hamacher, B. (2019, July 12). *'Dadeland Mall Massacre': Thursday marks 40th anniversary of infamous 'Cocaine Cowboys' shootout.* NBC Miami. https://www.nbcmiami.com/news/local/dadeland-mall-massacre-thursday-marks-40th-anniversary-of-cocaine-cowboys-shootout/127956/

Hamacher, B. (2017, April 13). *South Florida's most notorious 'Cocaine Cowboys.'* NBC Miami. https://www.nbcmiami.com/news/local/south-floridas-most-notorious-cocaine-cowboys/11254/

Harvey, A. (2023, December 27). *The story of Jorge 'Rivi' Ayala, the 'Cocaine Cowboy' who served as Griselda Blanco's top hitman.* ATI. https://allthatsinteresting.com/jorge-rivi-ayala

InSight Crime. (2024, March 15). *Sinaloa Cartel.* https://insightcrime.org/mexico-organized-crime-news/sinaloa-cartel-profile/

Jiménez, S. (2024, January 31). *La razón por la que Griselda Blanco quiso estrangular al último hombre que le rompió el corazón.* La Razón. https://www.larazon.es/internacional/que-griselda-blanco-quiso-estrangular-charles-cosby-ultimo-hombre-que-rompio-corazon_2024013165ba2ae3327cdd00019adedc.html

The Kings of Miami, la docuserie sobre los últimos "vaqueros de la cocaína." (2021, April 8). Clarin. https://www.clarin.com/espectaculos/tv/the-kings-of-miami-docuserie-ultimos-vaqueros-cocaina-_0_AzgOwgutU.html?srsltid=AfmBOoqZOzFIhoQm9TQRl1ynp5ohJK-deacssY4yhgY1Io5SgX4HWLIp

Kline, H., Garavito, C., Parsons, J., Gilmore, R., McGreevey, W. & the Editors of Encyclopedia Britannica. (n.d.). La Violencia, dictatorship, and democratic restoration. In *Encyclopedia Britannica.* February 20, 2025. https://www.britannica.com/place/Colombia/La-Violencia-dictatorship-and-democratic-restoration

LeGardye, Q. (2024, February 2). What happened to Griselda Blanco's husbands? *Marie Claire.* https://www.marieclaire.com/culture/tv-shows/griselda-blanco-husbands/

Luscombe, R. (2012, September 4). *'Godmother of cocaine' shot dead in Colombia*. The Guardian. https://www.theguardian.com/world/2012/sep/04/godmother-cocaine-shot-dead-colombia

La mansión del crimen: el destino incierto de la casa de Griselda Blanco en Miami. (2024, February 1). La Nación. https://www.lanacion.com.ar/estados-unidos/la-mansion-del-crimen-el-destino-incierto-de-la-casa-de-griselda-blanco-en-miami-nid01022024/

Matassa, C. (2024, January 27). *What happened to Griselda Blanco's sons?* Business Insider. https://www.businessinsider.com/griselda-blanco-sons-now-michael-blanco-lawsuit-netflix-2024-1

McGrath, M. (2016, March 8). *Nancy Reagan and the negative impact of the 'Just Say No' anti-drug campaign*. The Guardian. https://www.theguardian.com/society/2016/mar/08/nancy-reagan-drugs-just-say-no-dare-program-opioid-epidemic

Meisel-Roca, A. & Ricciulli-Marin, D. (2018, April). *La pobreza en Santa Marta:*

Los estragos del bien. Documento de Trabajo Sobre Economía Regional y Urbana. https://repositorio.banrep.gov.co/server/api/core/bitstreams/2723adc9-279e-4b5f-9b52-ffc73de18cbb/content

Miranda, B. (2017, April 26). *La reaparición de Augusto Falcón, el último "cowboy de la cocaína", que pasó escondido 26 años y es acusado de exportar toneladas de droga a Estados Unidos*. BBC

News. https://www.bbc.com/mundo/noticias-america-latina-39713985

Mitchell, M. (2021, August 4). *'Cocaine Cowboys The Kings of Miami': Where Are Willy Falcon and Sal Magluta Today?* Newsweek. https://www.newsweek.com/cocaine-cowboys-kings-miami-where-today-sal-magluta-willy-falcon-los-muchachos-netlix-1616051

Ovalle, D. (2024, February 1). *'Cocaine godmother' Griselda Blanco gunned down in Colombia.* Miami Herald. https://www.miamiherald.com/news/local/community/miami-dade/article1942420.html

Ponti, C. (2024, January 29). *Griselda Blanco: A blood-thirsty queen among the Cocaine Cowboys.* A&E. https://www.aetv.com/real-crime/griselda-blanco-poverty-to-wealth

Presnell, R. (2024, February 8). *Did Griselda Blanco and Pablo Escobar actually know each other?* Collider. https://collider.com/griselda-blanco-pablo-escobar-true-story/

queerstorian. (2019, October 5). *Griselda Blanco.* World Queerstory. https://worldqueerstory.wordpress.com/tag/fernando-blanco/

Ramírez Patiño, S.P. (2011). Cuando Antioquia se volvió Medellín, 1905-1950. Los perfiles de la inmigración pueblerina hacia Medellín. *Anuario Colombiano de Historia Social y de la Cultura.* https://repositorio.unal.edu.co/handle/unal/39466

Robinson, A. (2024, February 8). *Who killed Griselda Blanco?* Radiotimes. https://www.radiotimes.com/tv/drama/griselda-blanco-death-true-story/

Rufo, Y. (2024, January 26). *Griselda: Colombian 'Cocaine Godmother' given Hollywood makeover by Sofia Vergara.* BBC. https://www.bbc.com/news/entertainment-arts-67921672

Sáenz Rovner, E. (2007). The "prehistory" of marijuana consumption and growing in Colombia between 1930 and 1960. *Cuadernos de Economía, 26*(47), 205-222. http://socialsciences.scielo.org/scielo.php?script=sci_arttext&pid=S0121-47722008000100001

Samuels, R. (n.d.). Drug cartel. In *Encyclopedia Britannica.* February 20, 2025. https://www.britannica.com/topic/drug-cartel

The Sinaloa Cartel: An intel analyst's guide for travelers. (n.d.). Global Guardian. https://www.globalguardian.com/global-digest/sinaloa-cartel

Spence, N. (2024, February 9). *Griselda Blanco's three husbands - including the one she had killed - and the partner who survived her.* DevonLive. https://www.devonlive.com/news/uk-world-news/griselda-blancos-three-husbands-including-9090151

Spencer-Elliott, L. (2024, February). *Ok, what happened to Griselda's multi-million pound Miami mansion after she fled the city?* The Tab. https://thetab.com/2024/02/07/ok-what-happened-to-griseldas-multi-million-pound-miami-mansion-after-she-fled-the-city

Technological advances take airport X-ray scanners to the next level. (2022, March 20). Transport Security International. https://tsi-mag.com/technological-advances-take-airport-x-ray-scanners-to-the-next-level/

Tikkanen, A. (n.d.). Griselda Blanco. In *Encyclopedia Britannica.* https://www.britannica.com/biography/Griselda-Blanco

United States of America, Appellee, v. Griselda Blanco, Defendant-appellant, 861 F.2d 773 (2d Cir. 1988). (n.d.). Justia. https://law.justia.com/cases/federal/appellate-courts/F2/861/773/138342/

Why early childhood matters. (n.d.). NCDHHS. https://www.ncdhhs.gov/about/department-initiatives/early-childhood/why-early-childhood-matters

Wigley, L. (2024, February 8). *What happened to Griselda Blanco's three husbands? What we know about Dario Sepúlveda, Alberto Bravo and Carlos Trujillo's real lives.* Good to Know. https://www.goodto.com/entertainment/what-happened-to-griselda-blancos-three-husbands

Wolfsonarchive. (2019, July 11). *On This Date In 1979...* [Video]. YouTube. https://www.youtube.com/watch?v=IFLTLqO62G4